arco*colour*collection

houses

"In blue"

houses

Author

Francisco Asensio Cerver

Publishing Director

Paco Asensio

Proofreading

Carola Moreno, Tobias Willett

Although colour itself has no prescribed meaning it does manifest certain spiritual and aesthetic values and the importance of its architectural function, alongside form, line and texture, is a vital contribution to the shaping of our perceptions. Blue evokes coolness and light, the eternal duality of the sky and the sea, and despite their diverse geographical locations all of the houses in this volume, with the notable exception of Franklin D. Israel's "Arango-Berry House" in Beverly Hills with the formal evocation of its blue walls, have in common the backdrop of the sea and the blessings of the climate.

These dwellings are not intended to represent developments in late XX century enclosed urban architecture, but are second or holiday homes away from the city, attempting to combine luxury and contemporary technological advances with a sense of intimate communion with nature, marrying interior and exterior through a formal and chromatic logical continuity yet retaining a respect for the privacy that is demanded by the socioeconomic group who inhabit them.

The style is clearly Mediterranean, with a strong representation from Catalonia and the Balearics including two projects from Carlos Ferrater with his visual nautical motifs, and rich in traditional references, which are in turn balanced against the playful juxtapositions of Italian neorationalism, represented by Richard Meier, the clarity of line of the Bauhaus emerging through the indigenous traditional metaphors of Illias Papayannopoulos, or the dynamic expression of openness and split level space typical of Frank Lloyd Wright's "Prairie School" and exemplified here by Alexander Tzannes' spectacular achievement in the difficult terrain of Mackerel Beach, in Australia.

"In blue" may seem a contradictory title, given that most of the dwellings are white-painted and the furniture and decor relies on a chromatic interplay of primary, metallic and subdued natural colours and textures, but these houses inhabit a world of reflection suspended between the ethereal blue of the sky above and the intense blue of the sea below. The predominance of glass walls and French windows, balconies and terraces, pools and sunlit vistas of a sea horizon in contrasting shades of blue. And just as the sea reflects the sky so the shadow patterns on the white-painted structures stand out as deepest tints of blue stolen from a painting by Cézanne.

"In blue"

houses

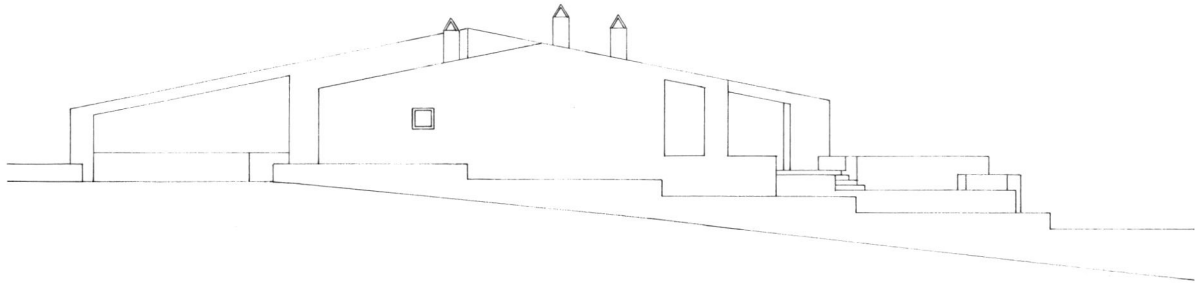

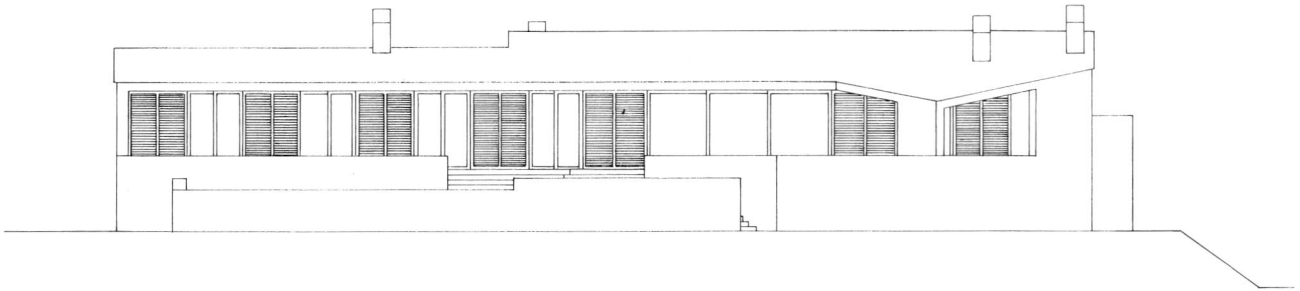

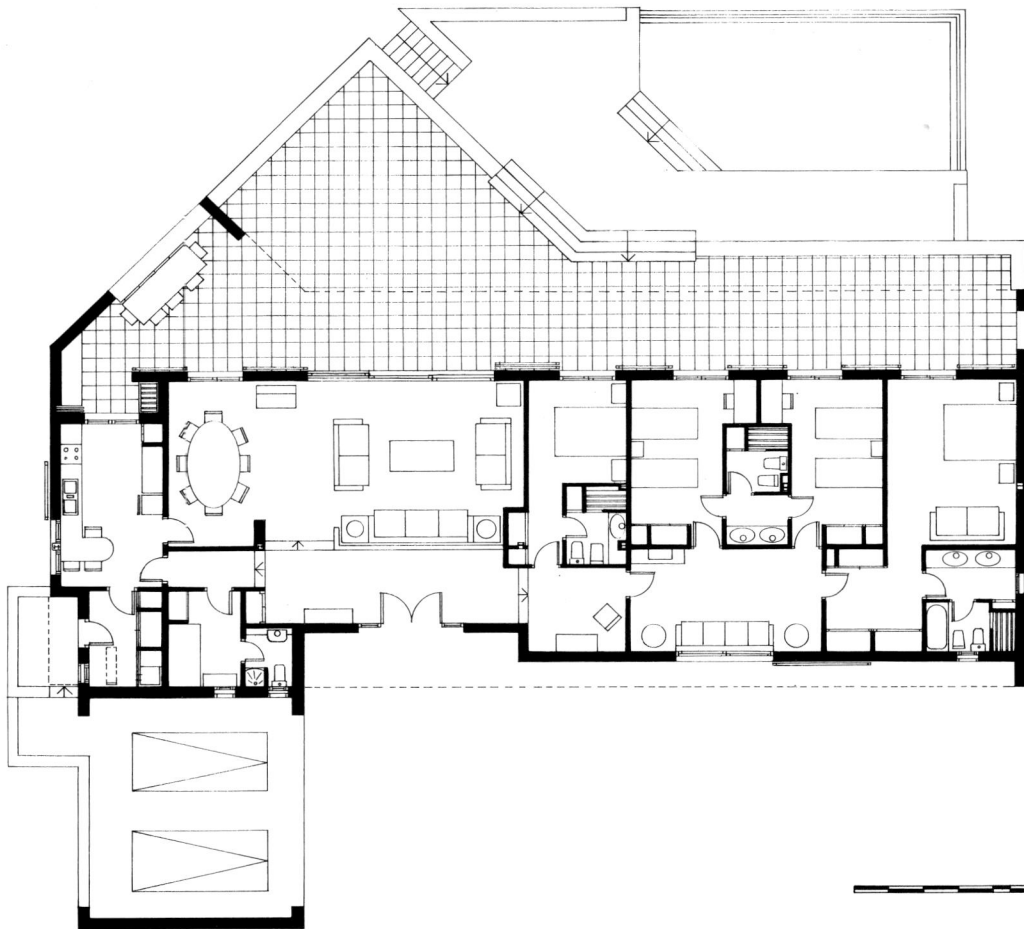

10

The dwelling's north elevation.

The dwelling's south elevation.

Plan of the lower floor.

Mediterranean light

Joan Maria Flores Casas

Single-family dwelling in Cadaqués, Girona (Spain) by Joan Maria Flores Casas.

One feature of Cadaqués bay on Catalonia's Mediterranean coast, a town of unique character due to the urban development surrounding it, and now of international renown thanks to the painter Dalí, is the abudance of olive groves around the old quarter. This beautiful region was the location for this single-family dwelling on a 6,000--m² plot.

The slightly rocky terrain, above sea level and surrounded by trees, lies some distance from the sea itself. The tramontana from the north is the prevailing wind, and in order to protect the house from this meteorological phenomenon the house was designed facing south.

Born in Barcelona in 1943, Joan Maria Flores Casas was the architect responsible for this project. He taught projects at the Escuela Técnica Superior de Arquitectura in Barcelona for five years, working in various fields of architecture, town planning and interior design. Among his most important pieces of work were the plans for several banks, such as Barclays Bank and the Banco Atlántico; in addition to single-family dwellings in S'Agaró, Santa Cristina d'Aro, Cadaqués and Alella, the interior design for the Aramis shop in Barcelona and a sports and social club in the Son Veri Nou residential area in Mallorca. He was involved in a joint project for a series of offices in Barcelona and is currently working on renovation projects of two buildings in the city.

The main exterior elevation of the building, painted white and with a Spanish tile, double pitch roof, looks out over the sea. In front of the enormous portico is a large swimming pool, which one reaches via a set of steps in the same colour as the floor of the portico, a shade of dark blue very characteristic of the deep waters of Cap de Creus. To take maximum advantage of space, the pool was built in a corner. The tiling is in white, Italian grained marble, thus breaking with the clearly defined visual line of the portico.

The design is an example of the conception of a Mediterranean house, in which one should highlight the simplicity of line and the manner in which it is incorporated into the landscape. A large number of

wooden framed windows with slatted shutters look out over the portico, all of which are painted white.

All the main rooms in the house have access to the portico, which covers over 30 metres with no supporting pillars, and to provide more space it is extended in a V-shape in front of the lounge. A rectangular pillar supports the section of roof covering the outdoor kitchen, creating a shadier area and an attractive windowed balcony enclosed by elegant railings.

The tiling on the portico is in brown flagstones, identical to those on the staircase, and helps to differentiate the two exterior areas of the main elevation. The rear elevation where the porch-cum-garage is situated, is more remote and has been completely

View of the side elevation, which is painted white and closes in on itself to a great extent.

View of the tiled staircase leading to the swimming pool area.

View of the tiled staircase leading to the swimming pool area.

whitewashed. Access to the interior layout is at the back, next to the porch-cum-garage. The roof has also been painted white, which makes the area brighter.

The hallway leads into the lounge-cum-dining room, a large space which opens onto the portico. The walls have been painted a shade of sienna to maintain continuity of tone with the stoneware porch and also to contrast with the interior woodwork and the ceiling, which are white. The floor has been laid with a textured carpet.

The furniture chosen was in the XVIII and XIX century Catalan style with Italian upholstery and curtains in a wide range of complementary colours. There are two very clearly defined areas: the dining room which leads into the kitchen-cum-office, with white stoneware flooring, white furniture and a large window which provides a

considerable amount of light. This in turn leads to the outdoor kitchen on one side, and a utility room and toilet on the other.

A small lounge was created in the bedroom area, giving the guest room a greater degree of independence. This leads into the television room, which helps separate the master bedroom from the children's bedrooms.

The latter are all symmetrical in shape and of similar structure. Both rooms open onto the portico and are connected by a shared bathroom between them. The floors of both rooms have a textured carpet which creates a cool atmosphere in the summer, whereas in winter it makes the rooms seem warmer. The floor in the bathroom was tiled in white stoneware matching the marble.

The paving around the pool is white bush-hammered Italian marble, in contrast to the flooring on the porch.

The swimming pool is located on a corner for maximum usage of space available.

The rectangular swimming pool and its small tiles.

The porch and the swimming pocl as dusk falls.

View of the porch, covered by the caves of the roof, from the swimming pool.

The dining room table in the foreground.

A bathroom and dressing room have been incorporated into the master bedroom. The walls, the floors and the interior design in general are in the same style as the lounge-cum-dining room. All the bedrooms open onto the portico and as a result Mediterranean light inundates the entire house, making it extremely bright. On the other hand the halogen lighting, with several independent circuits, enables the occupants to vary the intensity of the light inside and outside, according to their requirements. Looking at the house as a whole, one can see how all the rooms have been articulated on a single level, without reducing the independence and scale of the whole building.

This dwelling in the bay of Cadaqués by Joan Maria Flores was constructed in a typically Mediterranean style, both in its architectural layout and the variety of features incorporated and colours used.

The key feature is the exterior portico, which provides the structure for all rooms within the house, all of which open onto this terrace area, not only giving it character and strength, but also an exceptional degree of natural light, highlighting the white facade of this most favourably located property.

The large windows connect the porch to every room in the house.

The lounge contains XVIII and XIX-century Catalan furniture, with Italian upholstery and materials.

View of the dining room.

Bathroom in marble, with white tiling.

Detail of the all-white kitchen.

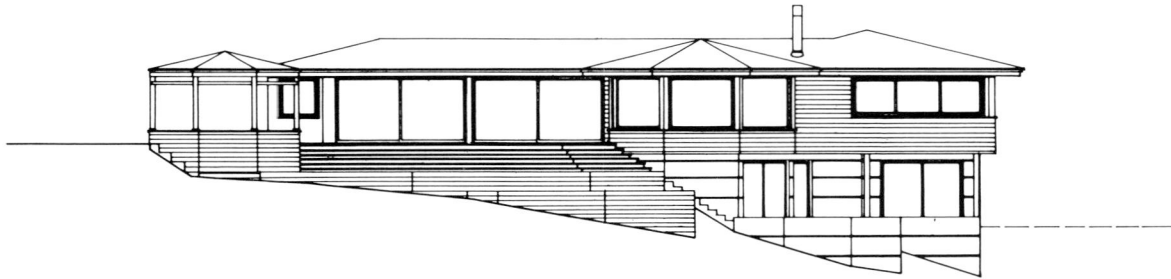

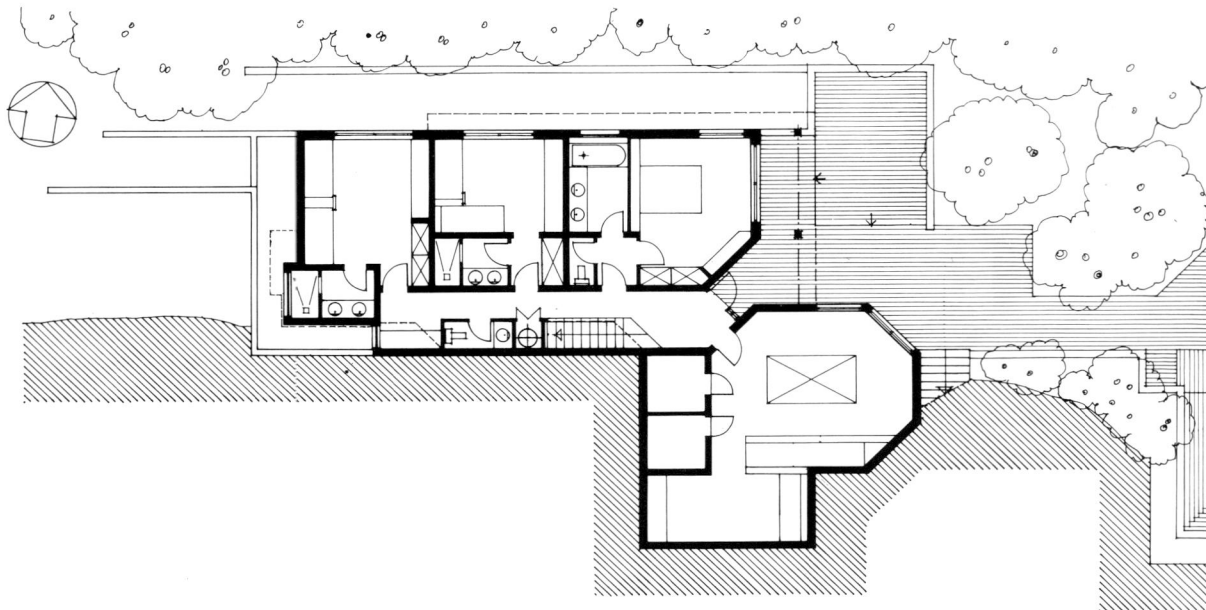

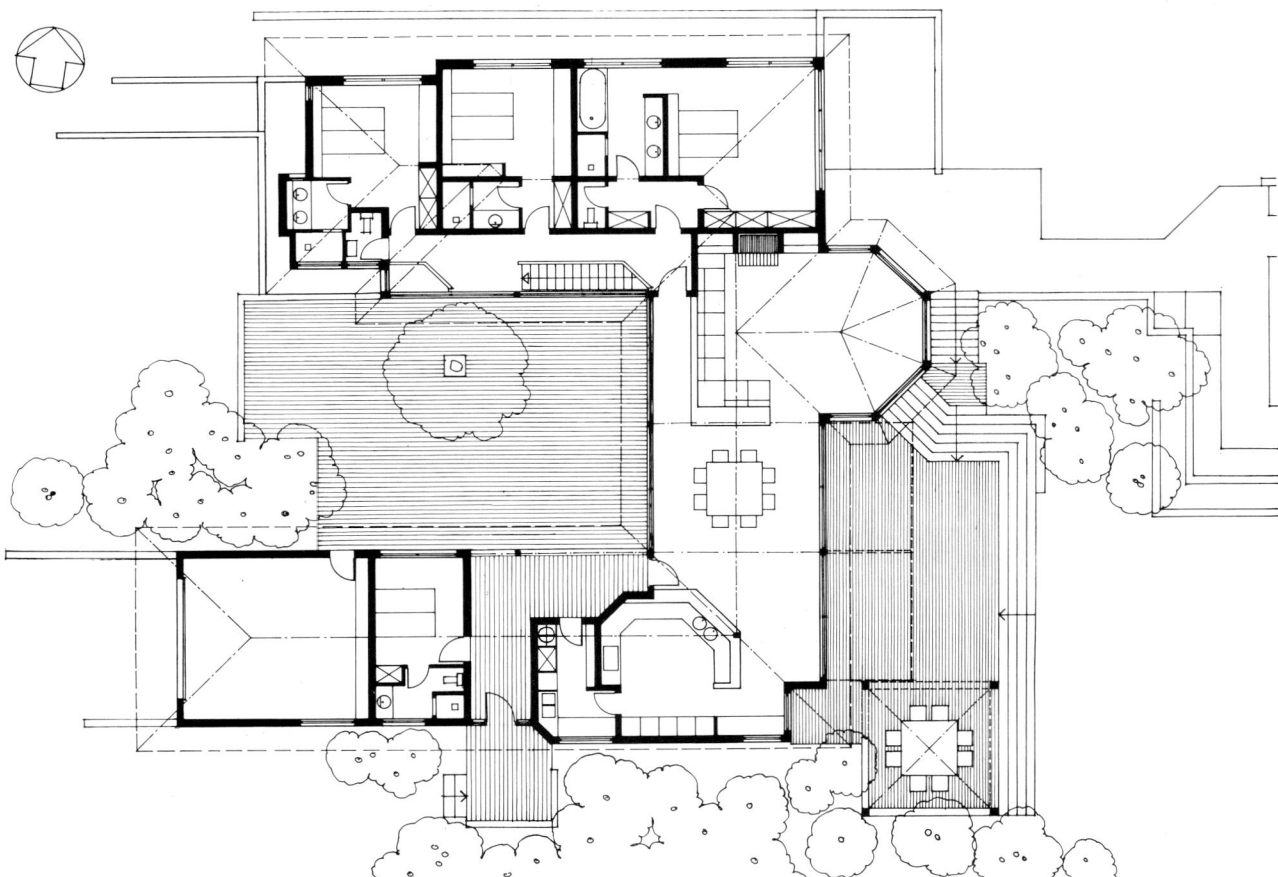

Architecture in wood

Guy Breton

House in Corsica, France by Guy Breton of the GEA Group.

This exquisite villa is situated in a residential area around a golf course at the southern end of the island of Corsica, France, beside the gentle cliffs of the Bonifacio Strait. This wood construction enjoys views of the Lavezzi archipelago and the island of Sardinia, allowing fantasy and imagination to fly while asserting its sober character, the architecture marvellously coexisting with the verdant landscape around it.

Built in red cedar imported from Canada, the house resembles a boat sailing wherever the wind may take it, towards freedom and holidays. It combines three essential elements: the conception of space, the views of the horizon and a trilogy of colours; white as in the sea foam, blue like the sky and grey like the command deck of a naval vessel. A ship with no obvious break between the interior and exterior, this house was designed for entertaining friends and letting the children enjoy their freedom.

Guy Breton, one of the four architects in GEA, Groupement d'Études Architecturales, was responsible for the design of this house. The construction was entrusted to the Société Insulaire de Porto Vecchio, managed by Lucien Longo and Italo Rizzo.

In 1969, after collaborating on the winter sports resort Avoriaz, four architects, Guy André Boguslaw Brezckowski, Jean Marc Roques and Guy Breton, created GEA. The most noteworthy of their projects are several tourist complexes, such as the seaside village of Ciappilli

23

A long wooden passageway runs around the
pool, accentuating the perspective.

and the planning of the island of Cavallo, both in Corsica;
the Quinta do Lago tourist complex in Faro, Portugal;
single-family dwelings in France and the Estoril Tennis
Club in Portugal. They also designed and built works for
local collectives in Propiano, Sarténe and Bonifacio and
subsided housing on the island of Abcan.

The 400-square-metre house is built on two levels on
a U-shaped plan. One side is extended towards the sea
by the terraces and swimming pool, while the other side
is more cosily grouped around an entrance patio watched
over by an ancient cork oak. The rooms in the house are
laid out around this central patio, protected against the
violent east winds, but open to the setting sun in the
west. In the middle of this space, a peculiar geometric
structure which houses the living room is the articulation

point of the ground floor. The entire building is of wood
and glass, both the upper and lower floors, letting in
abundant natural light that adds brillance to the interior
atmosphere and decoration.

The walls are clad with ventilated, red cedar siding,
and the overhanging roofs are covered with cedar
shingles, supported by a white wooden truss. On the
seaward elevation there is a terrace, which is a
continuation of the living room inside the building. It
functions as a second living room, and includes a dining
nook on one side of the pool at a slightly lower level.

The swimming pool is framed by a wooden border.
This deck and the benches on it are made of and
finished in the same red cedar used in the rest of the
house. To accentuate the views, one of the key elements

of this villa's architecture, a long path borders the pool on both sides.

The interior is also finished in wood, but painted white. This warm, noble material lends an elegant sobriety to the design. The interior decoration is resolved with elegance and simplicity in a chromatic interplay of blues and whites appropriate for a seaside house, which in this villa is distinguished by its beautiful and functional modern design. Along the access road, the south wing houses a service area, garage and kitchen. The daytime living area is in the central geometric structure, in a single, transparent space, open to the landscape and sheltered by the roof; an impressive living area including a lounge, dining room and kitchen laid out under a

superb structure and enclosed by sliding glass doors that link this space to the terraces outside. In the lounge, the simple furniture is of the same material as the house. Some of the furniture in this room is built into the white painted wooden walls, for example, the bookshelves, recesses and the fireplace. There is no barrier between the white and very functional kitchen and the lounge. The cupboards in the wall and the wooden counter are made to measure. The dining room on the other side of the counter also has wooden furniture, and the armchairs are upholstered with striped blue and white fabric.

The nighttime area is in the north wing. The bedrooms are on both floors off long corridors, reminiscent of staterooms on a boat. The two floors are connected by

View of the glass and wood sea facade. The lounge chairs of the sundeck are seen in the foreground.

The rectangular pool is framed with wooden planks.

Cedar has been used for the floor of this space and to make the benches and steps.

an exquisite wooden stairway painted white. The master bedroom communicates visually with the marine landscape and the pool. The children's bedrooms, simple and also decorated in white, have an informal design, and the guest bedrooms are more refined. The decoration is almost stark; the simplicity of the teak furniture, the refinement of the blue fabrics and the modernity of the built-in units harmonise perfectly with the architectural conception of this house.

This beautiful villa located beside the Sférone golf course on the island of Corsica in the privileged locality of Bonifacio was created by Guy Breton and the GEA Group. The design was based on three principal elements, one of which is its essence: red cedar wood. The house is cleverly designed on a U-shaped ground plan around the central geometric structure which houses the lounge. The design is enhanced by the long corridors in both the interior and the exterior, and the chromatic interplay between the luminous white of the wood inside and the blue of the decoration, echoing the colour of sea and sky. The shade of grey used is reminiscent of a ship's bridge, making the villa look like a boat allowing imagination and fantasy to fly towards freedom.

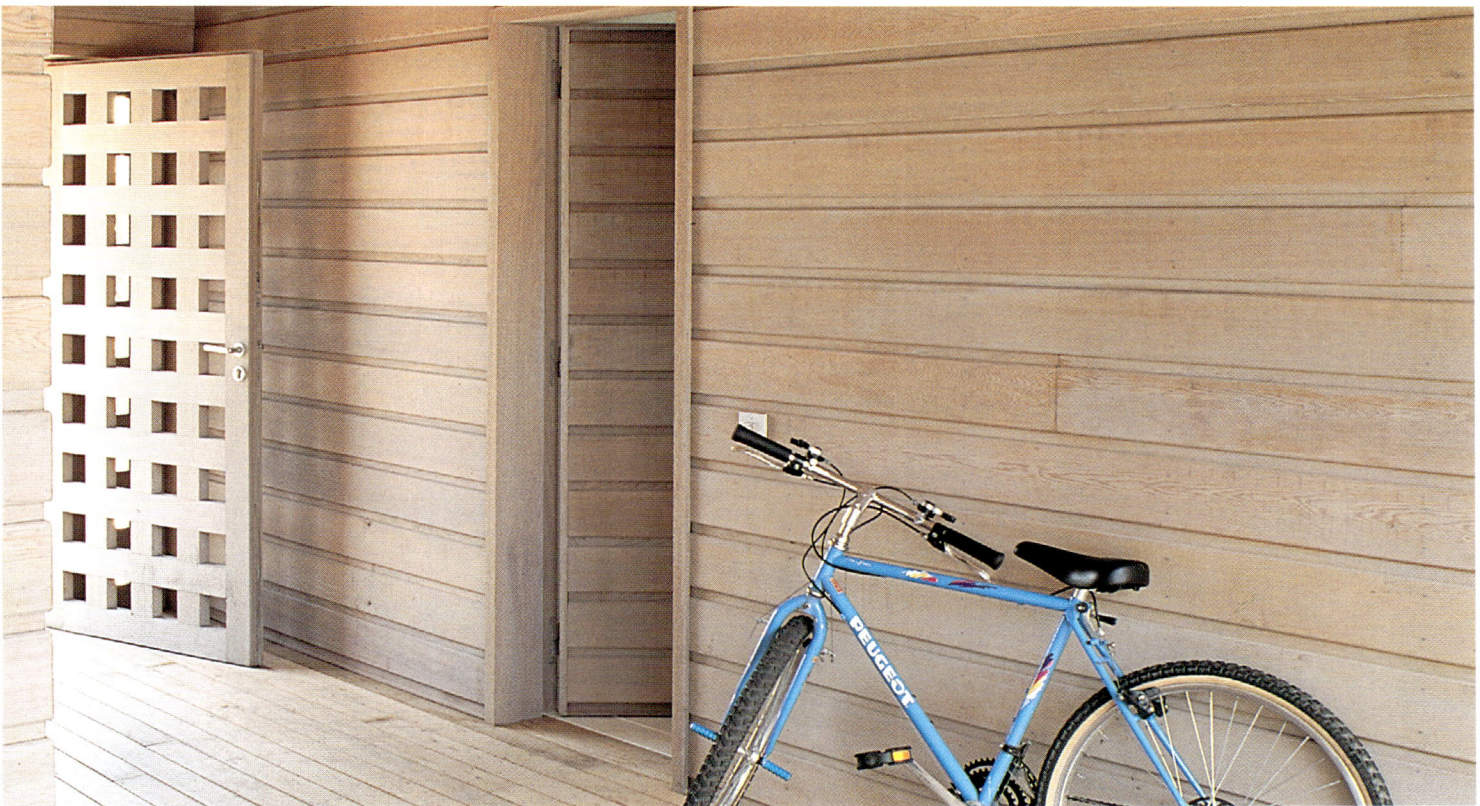

Interior room finished with cedar at the entrance to the house.

The living room is laid out beneath a massive structure, its glass sliding doors extending the space to the exterior decks.

The living room ceiling is painted white. The room opens onto the deck and the sea.

A wooden table with armchairs in the dining room, off the kitchen.

View of the master bedroom, which connects visually with the marine landscape and the pool.

The bathroom and shower unit are both completely white.

Perspective of the stairway leading to the upper level from the dressing rooms.

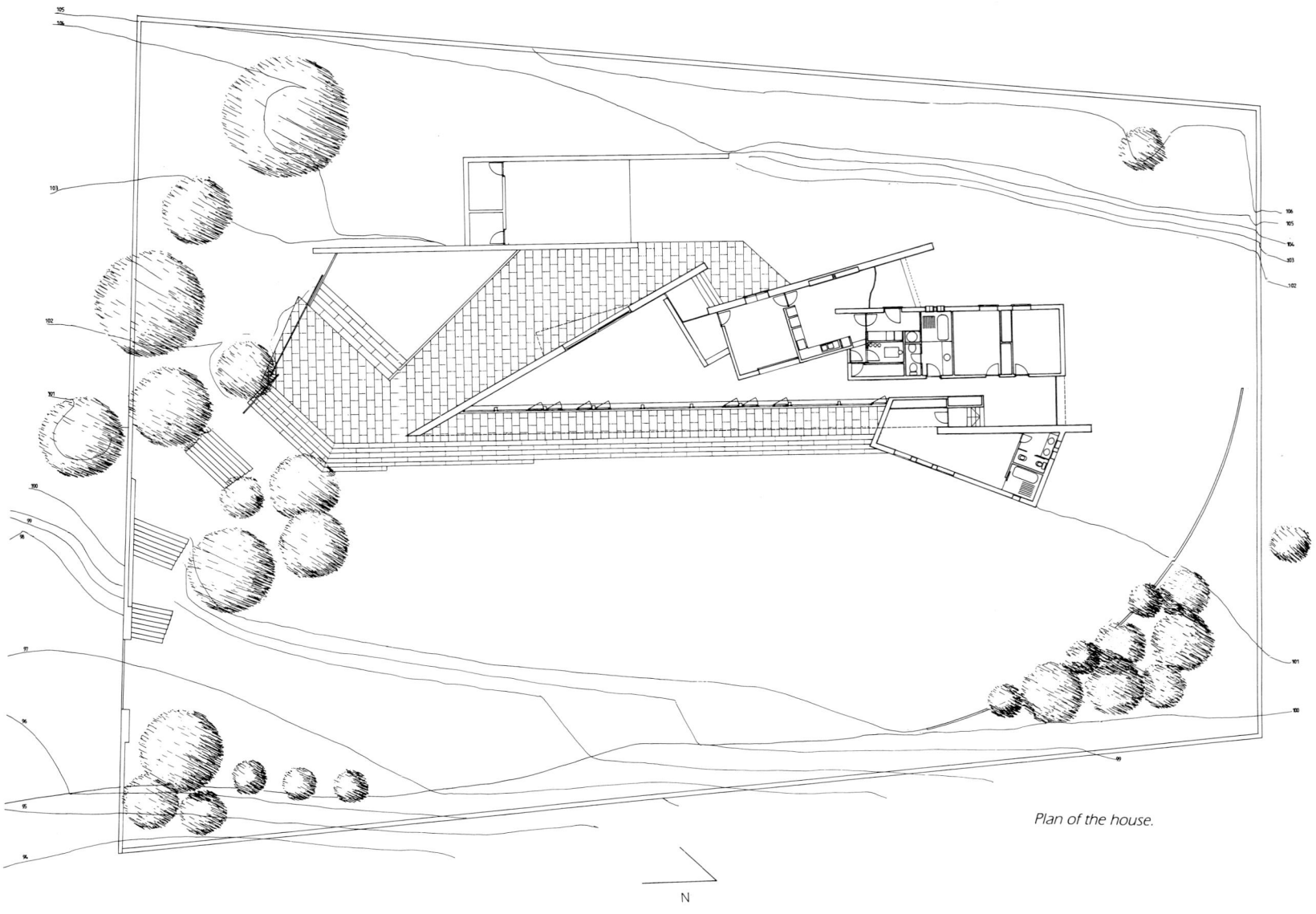

Plan of the house.

N

Open fan-shaped construction

Ignasi de Solà-Morales

This house, located in Aiguablava (Girona, Spain), has been constructed on a rectangular site, with a total area of 3,011 m². The long side of the rectangle lies parallel to the shore, overlooking the sea perpendicular to the north-south orientation. The site, previously a vineyard, has a constant slope of approximately 15% except in the southeast sector, where the inclination is steeper and the terrain runs down to the lane which gives access to the property from the Begur-Fornells road. The rest of the site has a total difference in elevation of seven metres beween the highest and lowest point.

Ignasi de Solà-Morales, who was born in Barcelona in 1942, is a doctor of architecture and has a Bachelor of Arts degree from the University of Barcelona. Since 1978, he has been head of the Department of Theory and History in the Escuela Técnica Superior de Arquitectura de Barcelona. He has been visiting lecturer at various universities in Spain and abroad, and has published numerous articles and books on architectural history and criticism. This house was shortlisted for the FAD prize for architecture and interior design in 1991 in Barcelona.

The architect has skilfully resolved the problem of the slope by constructing the building on an axis parallel to the sea running from north to south, which divides the site into two equal sections. The axial line, created by a row of pillars which, from a large portico facing the sea, defines the layout of the house in the shape of a fan. This fan shape goes beyond the house itself and is echoed in the surrounding tiled areas and terraces.

33

The glass main facade, showing the flat
concrete projecting roof.

The house is built along a north-south axis running parallel to the sea which divides the site into two equal parts.

The house was built on an irregularly shaped ground plan. View of the facade containing the main entrance.

The structure of the building is based on linear load-bearing walls 45 cm thick, arranged in the shape of a fan and covered with a large flat concrete roof, which extends to cover the main facade formed by the pillars. A smaller roof covers the main bedroom on a lower level.

The residence consists of two buildings: the dwelling, and an adjacent construction, half buried in the slope of the hill, which houses the double garage, a small machine room for the swimming pool and a cellar.

All the necessary rooms have been located on a single ground floor which is, however, divided into three successive levels. The entrance to the building is on the highest level where the dining room, kitchen and laundry are located. Sharing the same roof but down two steps, we find the living room, a corridor leading to the

nighttime living room, bathroom and two bedrooms. Finally, the master bedroom is down four more steps, under a separate roof which is at a lower level than the previous section.

Inside the house, Ignasi de Solà-Morales has clearly differentiated between the day area and the night area. The triangular sitting room looks out over the sea in the western wing, and on the eastern side it opens onto the terrace and the swimming pool. The trapezoidal pool is bordered by a wall covered with a blue mosaic which fuses with the colour of the water. This architectural element, besides forming the wall of the pool, provides a blue chromatic counterpoint which contrasts with the blinding whiteness of the walls of the house. The severe and simple design of the swimming pool is achieved by the use of a simple and, at the same time, very original layout, accentuated by the absence of ladders of a springboard. The pool is on the same level as the paved area around the house. This continuity gives the sensation of spaciousness to the different areas and creates an atmosphere of clarity and transparency.

The dining room is connected to the kitchen which, in turn, is connected to the laundry and boiler room. All these rooms, together with the hall, make up the daytime area. The night section is comprised of a main bedroom with en suite bathroom, and two other bedrooms which share a second bathroom. All these rooms are laid out around a living area. The two living rooms, situated one at each end of the house, together with the corridor which

links them, are in fact a single space, the result of the fan layout of the rest of the rooms and the facade, with respect to the axis of the west elevation, formed by the row of pillars.

The walls have been painted white, while the wood trim in the hall, kitchen and living room is painted in three high-gloss colours: blue, green and red, thereby highlighting the points of inflection between each of the three main areas of the house.

In the construction of this house Ignasi de Solà-Morales, in association with Gustavo Gili Galfette and Lluis Dilmè, has created a complex relationship between the architecture and its environment. This Catalan architect has demonstrated how, in architectural design,

The house consists of two buildings: the dwelling and a half-buried construction which serves as a garage and wine cellar.

Detail of the white bathroom.

The dining room is on the highest level, and opens onto the outside through floor-to-ceiling windows which create a clear and transparent atmosphere.

awareness and sensitivity towards the landscape and proper use of the topography of the site can constitute an ideal basis for producing a building which combines, as in this case, originality and functionality. The house opens out in the form of a fan, articulated around a virtual axis composed of a row of pillars which form a large portico facing the sea. This fan-shaped facade and the continuity of the spaces inside the house give the whole construction a transparent atmosphere and great luminosity.

The dark parquet floor in this bedroom is complemented by the orange and white walls.

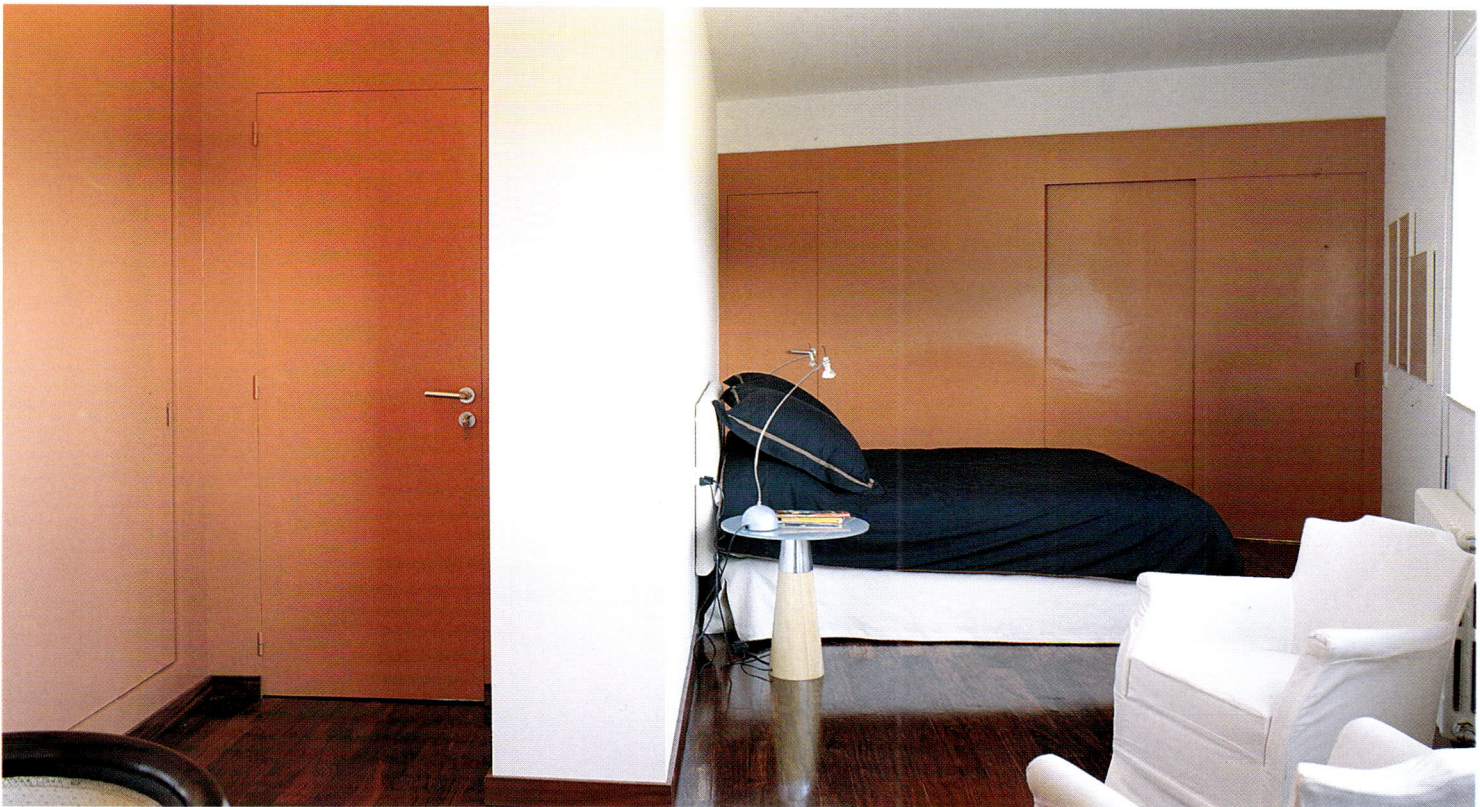

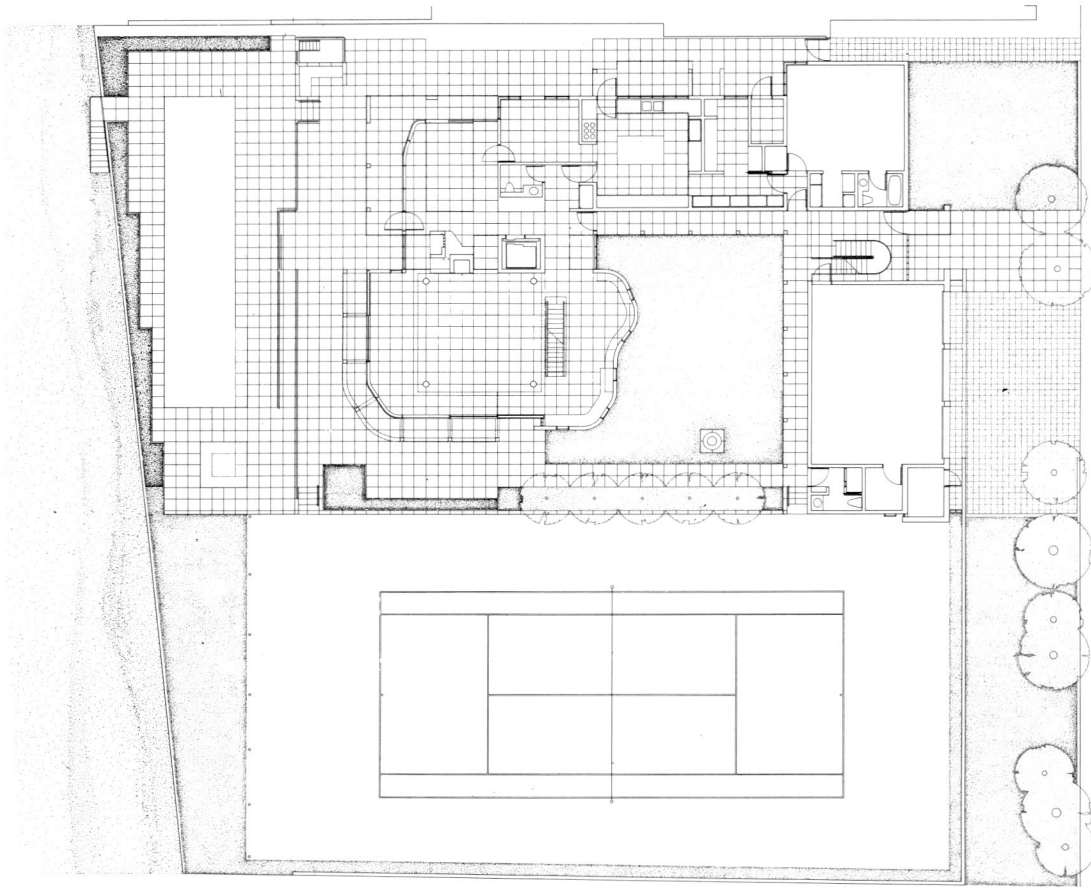

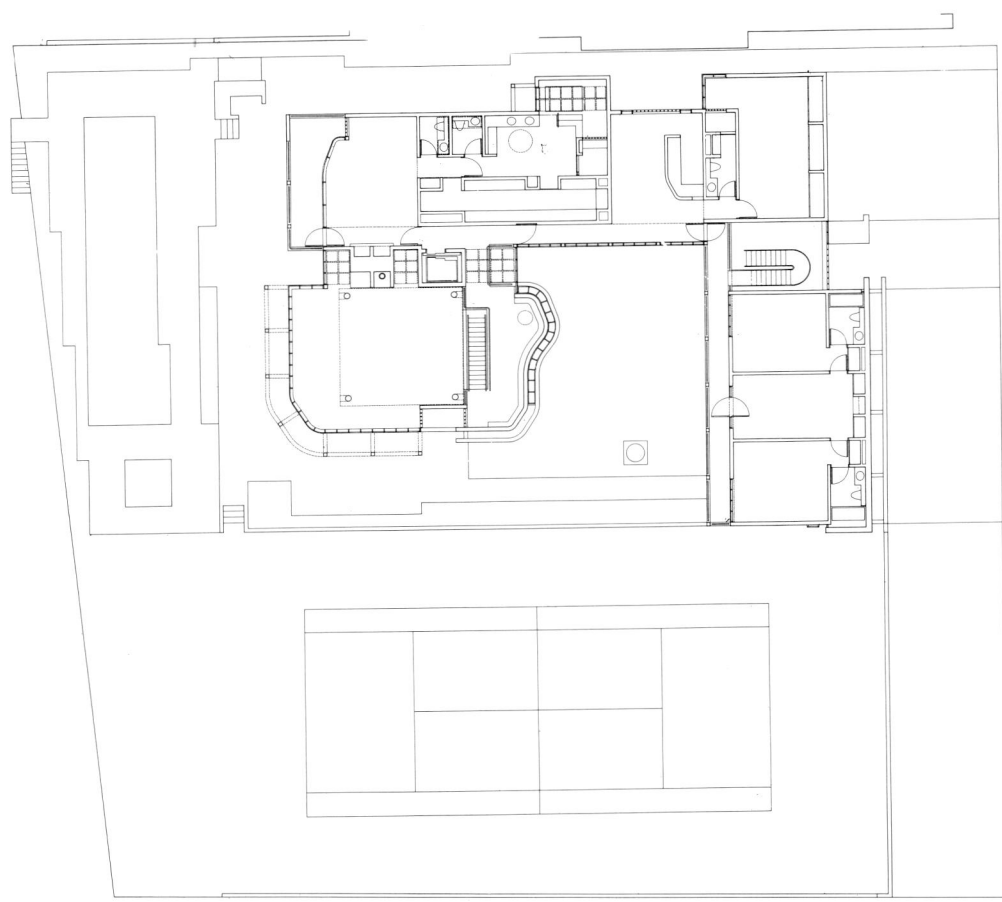

40

Ackenberg house

Richard Meier & Partners

A single-family dwelling in Malibu (California) by Richard Meier & Partners.

Related to the style of indigenous patios typical of southern California, this dwelling designed by Richard Meier & Partners aims at mediating between the mountains which stretch the length of the coast road and the beach which looks out across the untamed Pacific.

The land chosen for constructing this building consists of three flat and adjacent plots facing Malibu beach, California, enclosed by a mountainous region to the north and by the coastline and ocean to the south.

Richard Meier studied architecture at Cornell University. In 1963 he founded his own firm in New York and since then his professional undertakings have included dwellings, medical centres, museums and commercial properties. Meier has received numerous awards and prizes for his work; among the most notable were the Pritzker Architecture Prize, also known as the Nobel Prize for Architecture (1984), and the Royal Gold Medal, the latter from the Royal Institute of British Architects (1989), and many others. He has lectured at major American universities (Harvard, Yale, etc.), given a considerable number of lectures both in the USA and Latin America, as well as in Europe and Japan, and his work has been published in international books and magazines. Furniture, paintings, collages, architectural sketches and the design of objets d'art are all included in Meier's projects; his work has been exhibited throughout the world.

This dwelling is laid out on an L-shaped basis and is divided into two floors; the family area and the rest area.

41

Night view of the illuminated living room, which opens directly ontc an interior courtyard facing the sea.

Cross section of the house.

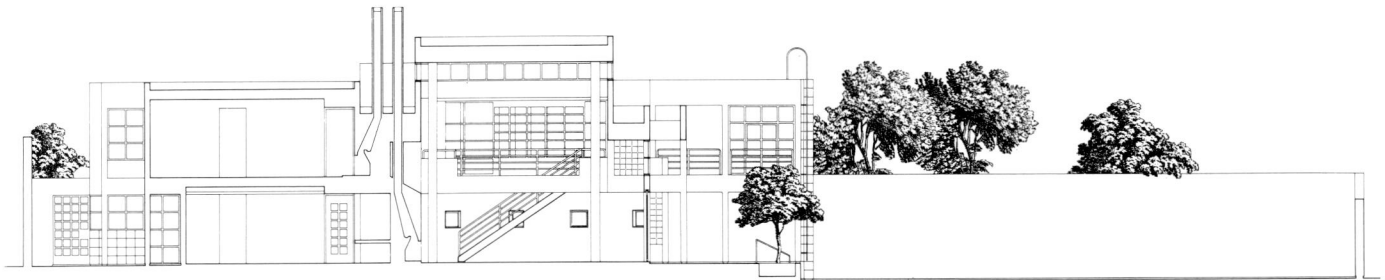

North elevation of the house.

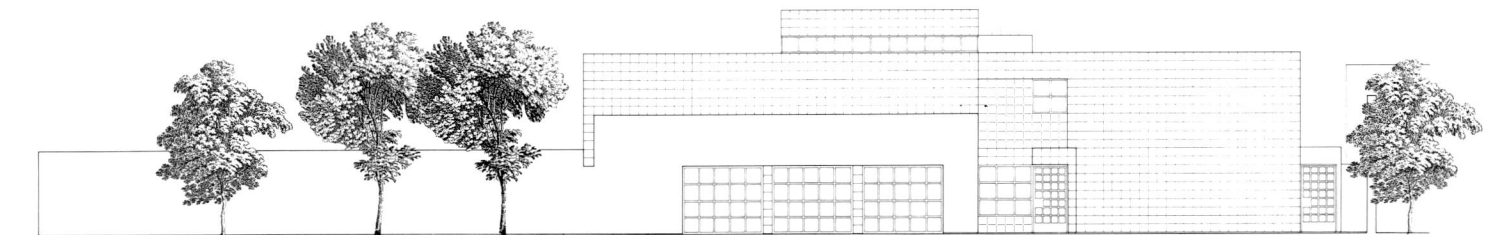

The main access is from the north side from which, passing through a covered hallway, one reaches a split-level vestibule with a glass-covered surface. This space leads to the large sitting room, dining room, kitchen and toilets, to the interior patio and the guest rooms. Ascending the stairs to the second floor, connected with the first floor by the open space of the sitting room, there is a suspended bookcase opening on to the lower level. Several bedrooms and a suite with dressing room and bathroom complete the basic layout.

This freely flowing spatial sequence is complemented by a previously existing tennis court, in the south section, and by a newly built, narrow swimming pool, on the west side.

As his principal challenge, the architect Richard Meier intended to create a considerable degree of communication between the exterior space and the interior of the building which, above all, would be established from the family rooms in the dwelling. For this reason the sitting room opens directly onto an interior sea-facing patio with magnificent views, which enable one to enjoy the marvellous climactic conditions of this temperate region. In reality, the majority of the surface area has large windows, reinforcing this spirit of spatial fusion, which was the architect's source of inspiration. Particularly at night when the house is completely illuminated, the glazing makes it appear almost entirely transparent, and thus definitively uniting the dwelling with

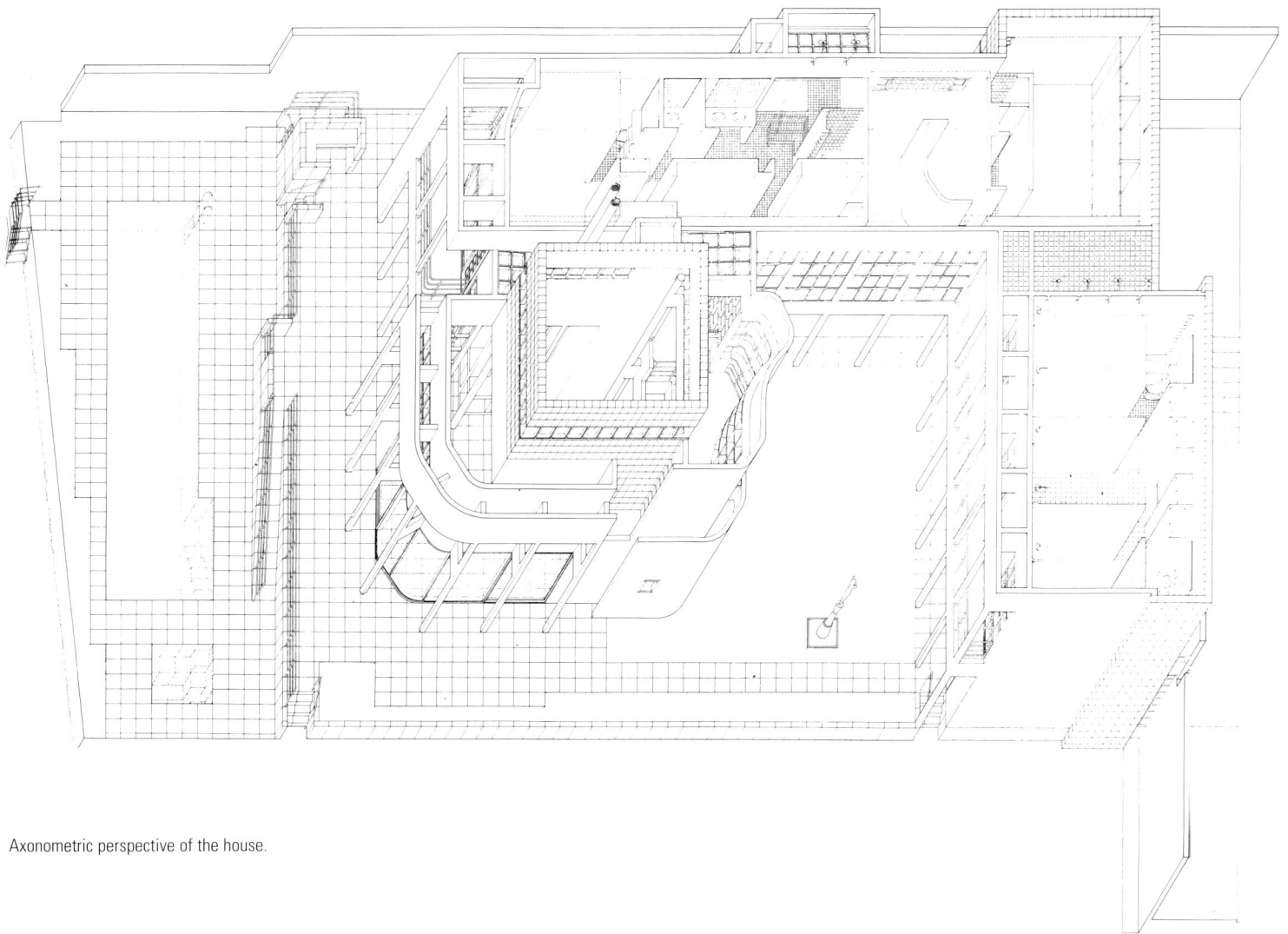

Axonometric perspective of the house.

The transparency of the interior is emphasised by the white wall and glass surfaces.

its surroundings. During the day, however, communication is established by a hedge which follows the line of the garden and acts as a break between the swimming pool and the sea horizon, contrasting the shades of blue.

Similarly, the materials and resources which are repeated inside and outside the property manifest, in a more specific manner, the same enthusiasm. Hence, the white metal handrails which mark the boundaries of the building and protect the balconies and terraces, complement the stairs, or that which can be seen in front of the bookcase, dominating the whole of the sitting room from above; a classical architectural component, the column, in circular or rectilinear form, was incorporated as one of the features which – from any perspective – gives this building a distinctive appearance. On the other hand, the whiteness of the walls and ceilings plays a leading role both inside and outside the house.

Another significant aspect of this project is the use of lattice work and skylights, which serve to modulate and control the ever-changing Californian light. As a consequence, excess heat and light are filtered, whilst inside there is an interesting play between shadows and reflections.

The rectilinear geometric forms, which dominate and characterise the whole of the structure of the building, contrast with the undulating wall in the sitting room, which opens onto the interior garden, producing a strange feeling of movement.

The use of glass on a large part of the surface area reinforces the spirit of spatial fusion.

Detail of the facade.

Two criteria were taken into account as regards the interior design: simplicity and comfort. Thus, the items of furniture respect the transparency and communication between the different rooms. The sofas and armchairs in the sitting room are of soft cream tones, on a similarly coloured carpet, surrounding a low marble table. The decorative elements which provide the brightest colours in this rather sparse and uniform whole are the pictures on the walls.

The ground floor has stoneware tiling, whilst on the first floor parquet has been used, indicating a separation between the family area and the bedrooms, which are slightly more intimate and welcoming as can be seen by the warmth of the wood as opposed to a colder and more impersonal sensation produced by the ceramic tiles.

The concept of an architectural design as a process of communication between the immediate environment and the surrounding landscape was what guided Richard Meier and his associates when constructing this single-family dwelling. Situated between sea and mountain, it took shape as an ensemble of flowing spatial sequences, freely and continuously related, giving itself over to nature and all the beauty that it is capable of creating.

The use of glass on a large part of the surface area reinforces the spirit of spatial fusion.

White buildings are a characteristic feature
of Meier's architectural philosophy.

Partial view of the facade containing the main door. The translucent walls filter the strong Californian sun.

Perspective of the white metal staircase which links the different levels.

The white and glass forms accentuate the play of light and shadow on the mass and void.

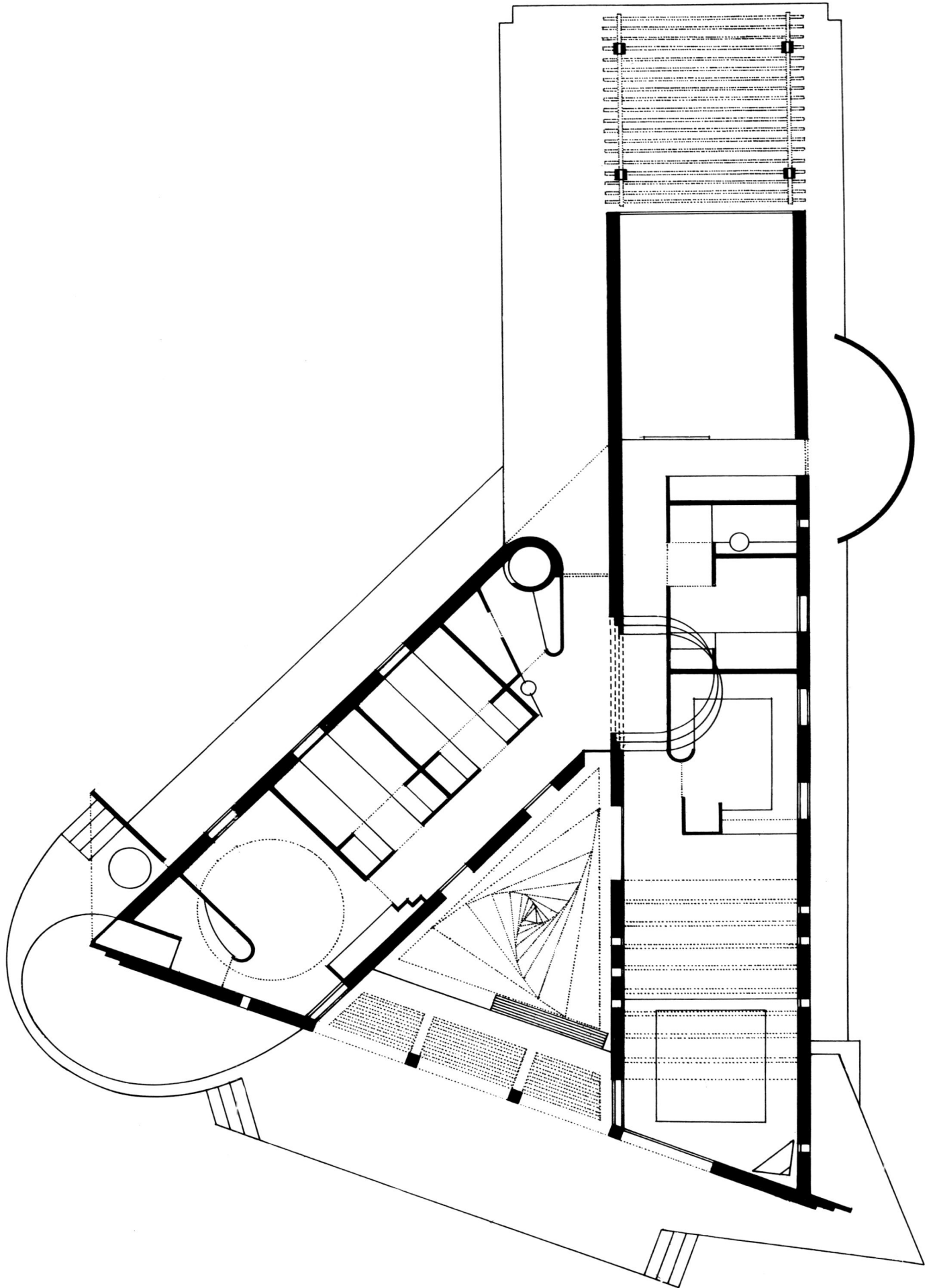

Traditions & new forms

Carlos Ferrater

This project by the architect Carlos Ferrater aimed at constructing a single-family dwelling, whose functional design was characteristic of a second home, with capacity for relaxation, far removed from everyday city life.

The property is situated in the south of Menorca between the geographical boundaries of Cap d'en Font and Binisafua beach, on the rocky coastline of a small bay flanked by several small islands. In this part of the island the properties are divided into large and narrow strips of land which are positioned perpendicular to the coast and separated by low, dry stone walls. The topography of the land, typical of the region, has significant irregularities and differences in levels because of its rocky nature, to which the basic structure of the house was suitably adapted.

Carlos Ferrater was born in Barcelona (Spain) in 1944. He graduated from the Escuela Técnica Superior de Arquitectura in Barcelona in 1971, the year in which he set up his own practice. He obtained his doctorate in 1987, and since then has been a lecturer, selected by means of competitive examinations; he currently holds the post of project lecturer for the sixth year at the Escuela de Arquitectura in Barcelona. Carlos Ferrater was president of ADI-FAD (1985-87), a member of the Senior Design Council (1986-87) and is currently president of INFAD. His work has merited prizes and nominations; a gold medal for the Aiscondel Pavilion at the Madrid agricultural show (Spain, 1973); a finalist for the FAD prize for interior design (1981); FAD award for the Opinión de Arquitectura (1982); a finalist for the FAD prize for renovation (1983); joint finalist for the FAD architecture prize in 1987; the Construmat'87 National Architecture Prize, etc. His work has been widely published in national and international specialist periodicals, books and magazines. The plans for this design were submitted in 1988 and it was concluded in 1990.

The building, of some 130 m², was developed on a one-storey ground plan and consists of two main volumes, trapezoidal in shape, which are positioned in two different directions and give it an oblique form, resulting in an open interior space which was utilised by incorporating a triangular patio. By so joining the two modules, the ground plan is given a Y shape, demarcating an open space which overlooks the porch and shapes the facade facing the sea. The front sections of both units are joined by means of a pergola which converts the facade into a continuous unit, the ends of which culminate in a tripartite arrangement. In this way the porch, which is reached by stairs positioned on the sides of the house, creates a unified front.

The entrance to the building is across the interior patio, which gives access to the corridors in both modules. The longest section, which forms a good visual perspective with the sequence originating in the sitting room, extends to the back elevation and has a portico supported on four columns. Situated in the other unit are the bedrooms and annexes and a cyllindrical volume, which juts out from the house, where one finds the solarium.

The extremes of the two volumes end with a three-part gradation. Perspective of the steps leading up to the veranda.

End view of the house showing the windows, set into the walls at irregular intervals to illuminate certain rooms.

The front walls of both constructions are connected by a pergola making the facade into a single continuum.

This project is part of a very specific architectural tradition which includes a sound and elementary volumetric definition, the play between the building and its environment. The design attempts to establish a two-way relationship. In order to solve the conflicts which such a design and construction entail, Carlos Ferrater used two fundamental strategies: the need to provide a structure consistent with the building and the uniformity of the land.

The unification of the plot and, in particular, of the ground plan, was achieved by using a continuous socle around the whole perimeter of the dwelling. Among Ferrater's objectives, one should highlight the homogenisation of the irregular surface on which the building was constructed and the incorporation of a

border which delineates the ground plan, shaping it as an intermediate space, at a point where the building is integrated with the utility annexes which surround it. At the same time, the socle functions both as a linking feature and as a border, which can be crossed in order to establish contact with the adjoining ancillary facilities. The base, built in Marés stone, provides the access – which gets round the unevenness of the elevation facing the sea by means of small stairways in the same stone – in addition to the pergolas, a small swimming pool and outside shower, a curved wall with a barbecue, access to the upper solarium, the patio and front porch.

In this way, a ground space is created with a varying geometry which adapts to the layout of the ground plan and the variety of service areas which complement it.

53

The curved wall situated beside the main building offers an unusual opposition to the long rectilinear perspective.

Facade giving access to the house.

Stairway giving access to the solarium on
the roof constructed in Marés stone.

A wooden bench in the interior patio.

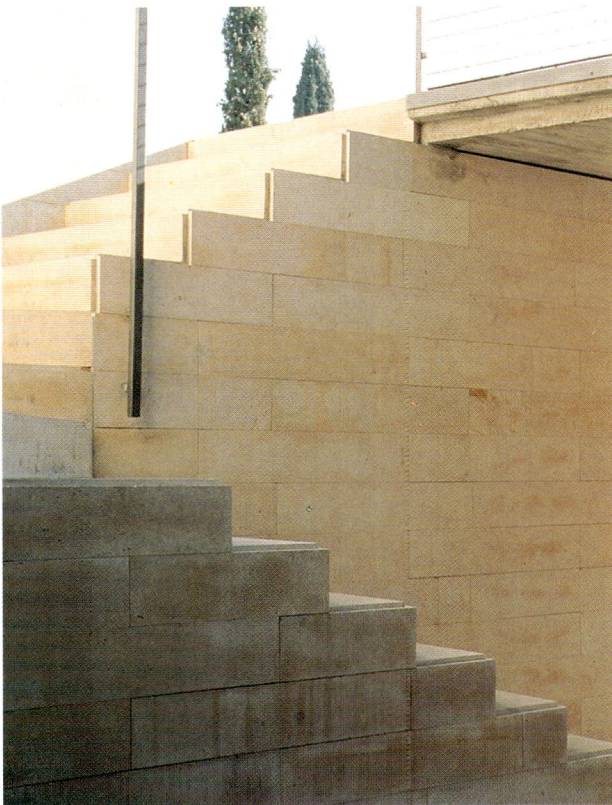

The visual perspective which the dwelling offers from the outside helps to decipher its internal features. On both sides the openings are positioned in a very exact manner so as to direct light to the most important rooms, such as the bedrooms or sitting room. The search for natural light is particularly concentrated in the patio formed by intersection, which is left uncovered in a vertical direction and only enclosed horizontally by the incorporation of a pergola, which follows the visual framework of the landscape. The distribution of openings on the interior patio provides indirect lighting in the corridors, which lead to the interior of the blocks, giving access to the other rooms.

Inside, the house sets up its own geometric dimensions, in accordance with the volumetric shape of the other units. The criteria for sectioning help to suggest the idea of movement. The additional facilities are mostly circular in form. The small swimming pool, positioned next to the front facing of the smaller block, has an unusual oval shape, broken by the walls. The curved wall alongside the main section makes an unusual contrast with the long rectilinear perspective and forms an imaginary passageway. Circular lines play a leading part in the cylindrical volume which serves as a solarium, rising above the building to catch the maximum amount of sunlight. The rigid geometric exterior form is softened by the undulations suggested by the additional facilities and has, at the same time, a certain air of modernity.

The interior design is worked out in precise detail, with few but necessary features: the washstand situated in the vestibule at the point of intersection, the small wooden bench on the patio and the unevenness of the latter and of the sitting room, and the halogen spotlights focused on the roof. All of which are complemented by the interior walls these are faced with scagliola pargetry and DM lining in varying tones of grey and blue. Likewise, the colour scheme is in harmony with the tones and materials used on the exterior. The house was built from 40 x 8 x 4 white brick, in the traditional style of the Balearic isles, and stucco work in colours which are normally found in Menorca, ochre, blue and sienna. The link between the materials used on both the exterior and the interior is equally apparent in the use of Marés stone, which unifies the external border of the ground

plan and was also incorporated to face the walls of the triangular patio.

The dwelling designed by Ferrater exemplifies a very personal way of combining the intrinsic values of an indigenous tradition with a modern and up-to-date rationale. The distribution of the physical spaces on the site aims to take maximum advantage of the natural light and capture the ideal visual perspectives. The basic criteria of the design adapt themselves to the formal masses in a style that is clean and pure.

Off each module follow the perpendicular contours of its walls. It is worth mentioning the solution found for the central section of the interior; the point of convergence was resolved by a series of three-way mobile arches

Nighttime view of the outdoor shower and the small swimming pool built against the side wall.

Detail of the main door, the wall and the outdoor shower.

Detail of the small oval swimming pool, the external veranda and the portico supported by several rectangular pillars

The swimming pool, built against the front wall of the smaller prism, has an unusual oval shape.

The search for clarity is constructed in the open-air patio formed by the intersection and bounded on one side by the pergola.

Detail of a hand basin situated in the hall at the point of articulation.

Partial view of the split-level living room and the large picture window, which commands a splendid view of the countryside.

The interior wall is finished with a smooth coat of rendering and moulding plaster painted various shades of grey and blue.

which are positioned at the intersection of the corridors, forming an empty space which serves as an informal vestibule for the external entrance to the smaller block. The air conditioning apertures and vents cross forming currents which penetrate the building from the interior patio.

Despite the predominance of straight lines and strict divisions, the dwelling does not give way to the illusion of symmetry. The forms are full of vitality and energy. The most obvious examples are the main facade, with its slight slope dictated by the intersection, and the interior patio in the shape of an asymmetric triangle. The severity of the straight lines is not exclusive. Using contrast, the curves help to suggest the idea of movement. The additional facilities are mostly circular in form. The link

between the materials used on both the exterior and the interior is equally apparent in the use of Marés stone, which unifies the external border of the ground plan and was also incorporated to face the walls of the triangular piano.

The dwelling designed by Ferrater exemplifies a very personal way of combining the intrinsic values of an indigenous tradition with a modern and up-to-date rationale. The distribution of the physical spaces on the site aims to take maximum advantage of the natural light and capture the ideal visual perspectives. The basic criteria of the design adapt themselves to the formal masses in a style that is clean and pure.

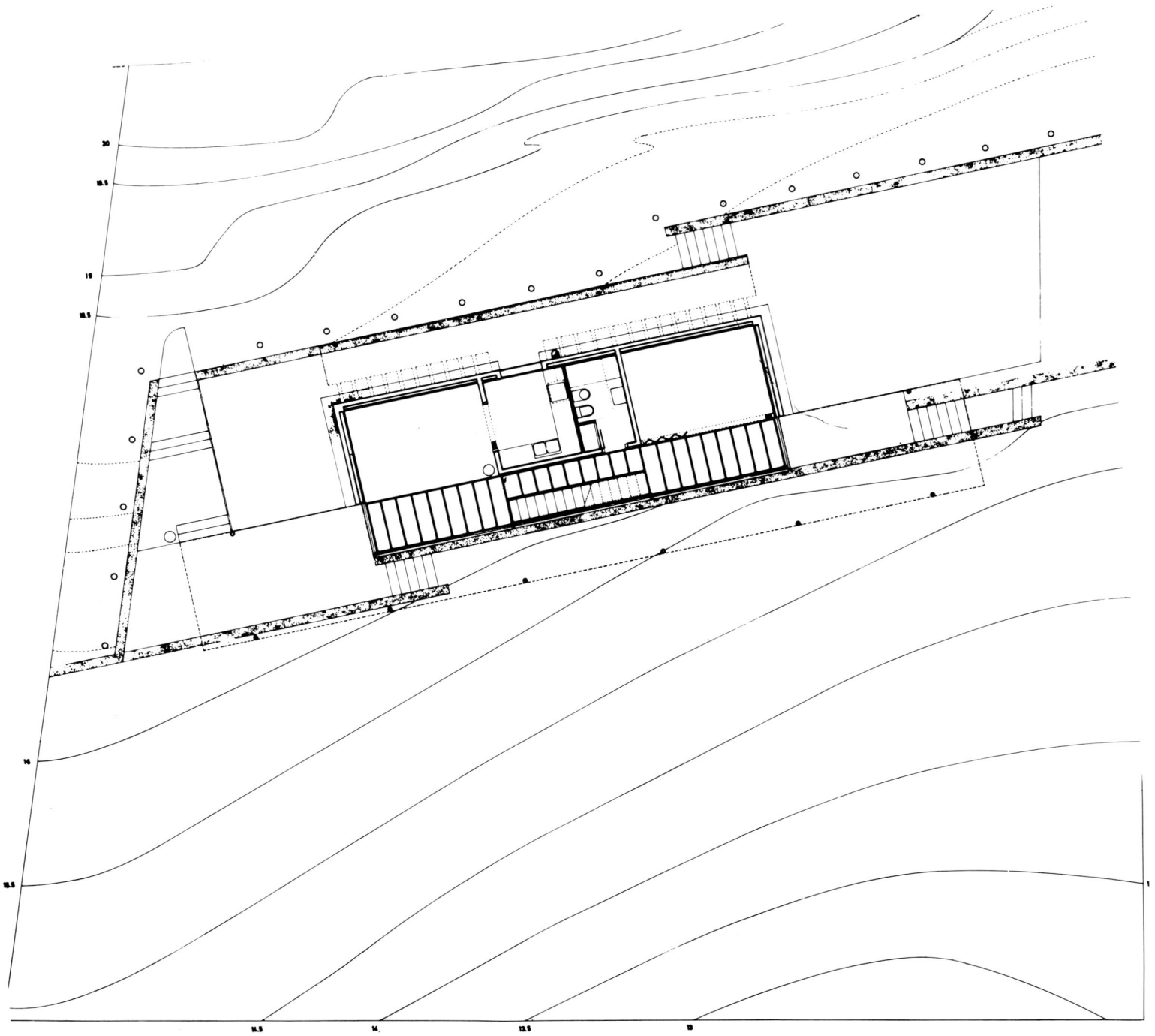

Emphasis on areas of movement

José Llinàs Carmona

House on the Costa Brava, Girona (Spain) by José Llinàs Carmona.

Several important factors influenced the design of this original house by José Llinàs Carmona. Chief among them was the importance its future occupants attached to life in the open air. Other conditioning factors included: the eastern orientation of the site affording a view of the sea and the land sloping down to it; a road running past the site to the west; financial constraints on the project; and the owner's preference for freedom of movement throughout the house over enclosed spaces.

The single-family dwelling is set on a small site (only 1000 m²) atop a hill on the road to Sa Tuna on the Costa Brava. A series of obvious conditioning factors were related to the terrain: the pronounced slope of the land;

its eastern orientation; the splendid sea views visible from one end of the site; and finally, on the more elevated, opposite end of the site, access from the busy road leading to the beaches, which defines the site's western boundary. This house adapts itself perfectly to these conditions and even uses them to its advantage.

José Llinàs Carmona, who drew up the plans for this building, received his doctorate in architecture in 1969. He taught at the Escuela Técnica Superior de Arquitectura in Barcelona for almost 20 years, from 1970 to 1990. He also held a similar position at the Escuela Técnica Superior de Arquitectura del Vallés from 1983 to 1990. This house on the Costa Brava was constructed in 1980.

The house is built on a flat paved area between two low retaining walls so that it can be entered from two sides. It

Perspective of the glassed-in gallery, which
fulfils the owner's desire for open-air living.

The west facade has very few windows, just
enough to allow sufficient ventilation.

is connected to the exterior by two terraces, with opposite orientations towards the sun. A path running around the rear of the house between the building and the retaining wall connects the two terraces and also is accessible from the kitchen, which has its own door. Inside the house, a gallery connects the six main divisions of space, establishing the relationship between interior and exterior. This gallery is the key element of the building's design.

This unusual house is a two-storey construction on a rectangular base. The ground floor includes the dining room, only separated from the kitchen by a sliding door, and the main living room. The upper level includes a cosy living room with fireplace, and the bedrooms. A stairway in the gallery connects the two floors.

José Llinàs Carmona's design was based on the idea of seeing this residence as an auxiliary building dependent on another hypothetical, nonexistent house with all of the conventional attributes of a family house.

One of the features which defines this work is that freedom of movement within the house is valued above any consideration regarding the division of the space into rooms. Perhaps the most important decision in this respect was to locate the internal connecting spaces, not in the rear of the house as was originally planned, but instead along the main facade, giving this area a privileged orientation commanding a splendid view. The distinction between these two clearly differentiated spaces, the access areas or passageways on the one hand and the

The entire front of the house is protected by a high metal pergola.

rooms on the other, is emphasised by the use of two different systems of construction The structure of the rooms is based on load-bearing walls and brickwork curtain walls, whilt the communication gallery has a structure of pillars and metallic beams with glass curtain walls. This steel structural shell also projects out from the house supporting a slatted wooden roof which shelters the large expanses of glass in the eastern facade. The materials used inside the house are also varied to distinguish the two areas. On the first floor, for example, the floors are wood in the communicating corridor but ceramic in the rooms, giving the passage areas a warmer, more pleasant quality. On the ground floor, on the other hand, the gallery is floored with large, light grey, ceramic tiles in contrast to the kitchen floor covered in smaller vitrified tiles in a darker shade.

The glass gallery also perfectly fulfils the owner's explicit desire for life in the open air since it allows an abundance of natural light into the house, and brings it into almost complete communication with the immediate surroundings and the landscape stretching into the distance. It is therefore clear that the only possible orientation was towards the east commanding a beautiful view of the Mediterranean, whose intense blue stands out against the nearby greenery of the thick surrounding vegetation. In contrast, on the west side where the view is of little interest there are very few windows, only those which are essential for adequate ventilation and minimum sunlight. In fact, a single narrow window crossing the rear wall is sufficient to carry out these functions.

The connecting gallery has a structure of pillars, metal beams and glass walls.

The steel reinforcement of the gallery extends outwards and supports a wooden-planked roof.

Partial view of the corridor and living-room fireplace.

Detail of the upper-storey corridor.

Dining room on the ground floor, connected to the patio with summer dining room.

Perspective of the stairway connecting the two levels viewed from the gallery.

The intimate living room on the first floor
features dark ceramic floor tiles.

In order to prevent a possible excess of sunlight, which could occur very easily in the pleasant, although at times extremely hot, climate of this region, the whole front of the house which is directly exposed to the sun, is protected by an enormous, grey metal pergola. This structure both protects the construction and creates pleasant shady areas around the house. In addition, all the windows are protected blinds which carry out the same function.

On one side there is a patio partially covered by a structure which projects out over the door, also in grey metal. This area, often cooled by the pleasant sea breezes and furnished with a table, is ideal for al fresco dining.

Outside the house the combination of the lawn, which covers a large part of the available space, and the terrazzo paving produces an intense colour contrast.

The interior of the building has been decorated mainly in white, which has been used on most of the walls and ceilings. In some places this is complemented by teak wood details. The furniture is sparse, thereby maintaining the clean lines and transparency of the interior spaces.

The building designed by the architect José Liinàs Carmona is marked by the intention that all of its implicit or even hidden aspects should create a dwelling whose true character could be brought out without any cumbersome restrictions. However, since the greatest importance has been attached to the areas dedicated to free movement and access rather than to the rooms as such; the privacy of its inhabitants has nonetheless been guaranteed, while they enjoy the constant opportunity of freely relating to their privileged surroundings.

The spacious master bedroom has smooth white walls.

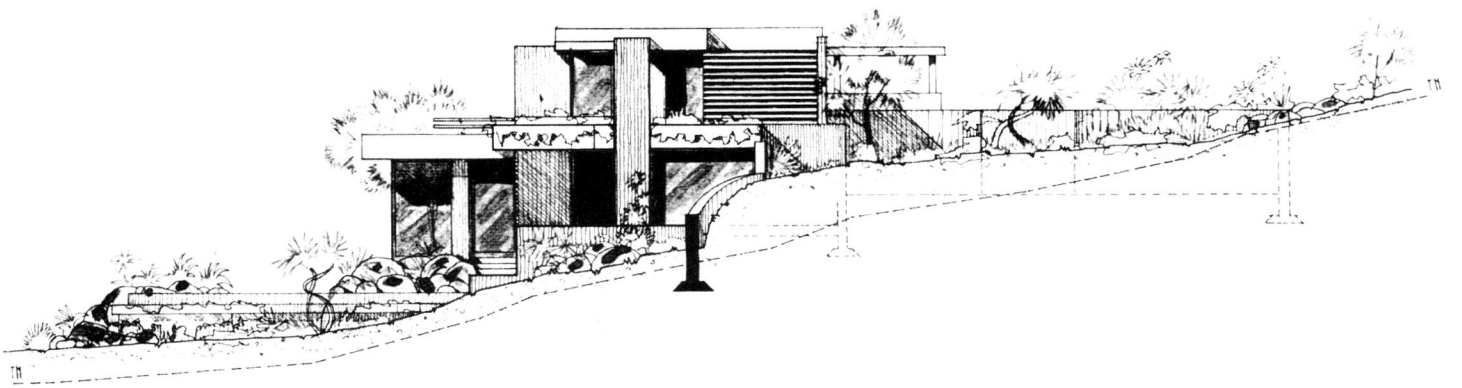

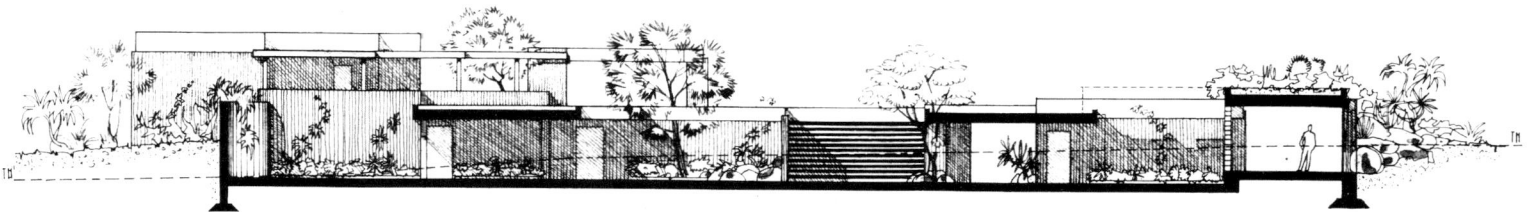

Symbiosis between exterior and interior

Luc Svetchine

Single-family dwelling on the island of Réunion (the Mascaregnes archipelago in the Indian Ocean) by Luc Svetchine.

Taking advantage of the truly exceptional landscape in front of the site selected for this house, the architect Luc Svetchine decided on a dwelling which would offer total communication and interpenetration between the interior and exterior space, and this characteristic finally became the raison d'être and chief determining factor in this project.

This single-family dwelling is set on a steeply sloping site overlooking the Indian Ocean, on the island of Réunion. The topography of the terrain led the architect to a design solution for this house based on a stepped structure facing the seascape. The orientation of the

house affords the inhabitants a truly exceptional panoramic view of the extensive coastline.

Luc Svetchine was born in Nice in 1956. In 1974 he enrolled in the École d'Architecture de Versailles, and he received his degree from the UPAM in Marseille-Luminy in 1981. Upon completing his training, he began his professional career designing and building private residences, housing developments, hotels, the Tourettes International Golf Club, and summer houses. His work even includes the renovation of a castle. He complements his activity as an architect with work in the field of design, creating contemporary furniture of the basically functional type, such as living room and dining room tables, console tables, bedside tables and rugs. He is currently building a group of houses along the lines of

Elevation of the house.

This way of extricating the frame of the building and bringing it forward into the open also serves to disconnect the curtain wall from the actual structure.

The swimming pool appears to overflow into the sea, creating an unusual visual effect connecting the two surfaces of water.

The topographical peculiarities suggested to the architect this stepped structure facing the landscape.

The view is split into rectangles by the multiple frames formed by the masonry and metal structures in the foreground.

a traditional Provençal village. This development, on a 3,000-square-metre site, will include a reception area, a large number of apartments, guest apartments and a group of secondary constructions to house the services.

The defining conception of this dwelling is an emphasis on transition areas: the paths, gardens and rocky areas which define a free but divided habitat, always offering a choice between privacy and sociability. The areas for entertaining guests are in the centre of the building, and the rooms are laid out around this point, as satellites of the central space, more or less close by, yet autonomous.

The main entrance at the rear gives direct access to the kitchen and its service areas, located just to the right, while a few steps lead down to the large living room at the front and the dining room beside it. The bedrooms are on either side of this central nucleus: the master suite to the left, and the other double bedrooms on the other side. All the rooms on this level open out onto covered terraces which feature a summer dining room, and many little nooks, ideal for enjoying a quiet rest. The upper floor is reached by a flight of steps built into the exterior at the rear of the house. This level, which is much smaller, was designed as an independent apartment for guests; it includes two more bedrooms, a living room and a terrace.

An independent structure in the garden is used as a recreation room. The paths leading to the pool have been constructed like the bridges of a ship. The juxtaposition of the swimming pool and the sea view produces a

Detail of a lateral facade overlooking the landscape.

Detail of the banisters. All of the trim is black anodised aluminium.

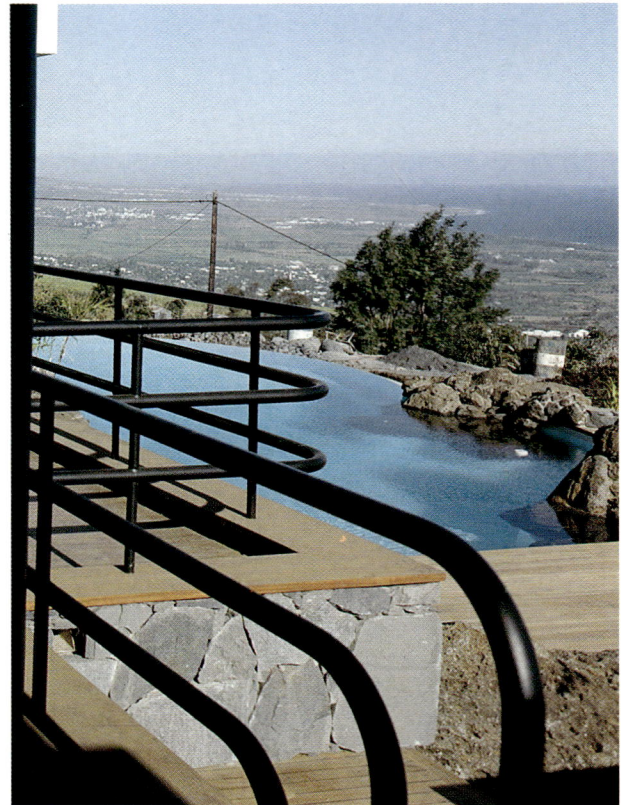

striking effect of visual connection between the two planes of water.

The exceptional panoramic view of a stretch of coastline over 10 kilometres long inspired Luc Svetchine with the idea of dividing up the view by creating multiple frames with the solid brick and metal structure occupying the foreground. This way of extricating the frame of the building and bringing it forward into the open is also a way of disconnecting the curtain wall from the actual structure. There is no continuity between the masonry and the glass surfaces; on the contrary, the sense of freedom conveyed by the line of the roof produces an effect that makes observers constantly doubt whether they are inside or outside the building. This intentional ambiguity is also related to the local lifestyle and climactic conditions.

This is so much so, in fact, that the interior volumes of the rooms make no sense without the complementary exterior space that forms an integral part of them. The architect's decision to use identical materials for the floors, ceilings and walls, inside and outside, stemmed from his understanding of this reality and his desire to perfectly connect the two spaces. It is also difficult to detect the difference between the interior and exterior patios since they all follow the sinuous lines of the structure and are decorated with the same sort of vegetation. This method of ventilating the house by introducing nature into the heart of the dwelling also lets the whole ensemble breathe, in every sense of the word, including that of inhaling the perfumed aroma of an incredibly exotic tropical flower.

View of the facade facing the pool and garden.

View of the glass facade and swimming pool. The garden existed before the house was built, and was integrated into it.

View of the swimming pool from the first floor. The rocks integrated into the pool give it a natural effect.

It is clear, therefore, that besides resolving the problems of layout in an unusual way, this architectural work deals with the question of protection from the sun and ventilation in a natural way, so that the house is fitted with neither heating nor air conditioning. This is common in these latitudes where the budget is frequently insufficient to cover this installation. Unfortunately, however, when the budget is available, the owners and architects too frequently tend to opt for the artificial solution, even when the very concept of the building makes this unnecessary.

The garden is designed to create the impression that it was not contrived or designed; it looks like the natural vegetation which existed before the house with only slight modifications.

The doors between the rooms are of an original design; full height, without handles or locks, they are operated by an electrically controlled shaft mechanism. The doors to the built-in wardrobes are both enclosures and mirrors. They are also free of superficial fixtures which adds to their great visual sophistication. In order to eliminate thresholds in the window openings, small recesses built into the supporting frames ensure the same level between the interior and the exterior.

The mechanical shutters can be completely retracted into a box in the tiled concrete so that they are completely invisible from the upper part of the window to the ceiling; this makes it possible for the plane of the interior ceilings to flow into that of the exterior without any kind of break.

The roof is flat and uninterrupted.

Glassed spaces in the interior afford a view
of the sea.

The rocks help integrate the house into its
surroundings.

The bathroom is finished with grey flooring, opium-coloured ceramic tiles and Burgundy marble.

Detail of the entrance stairway.

Detail of the glass dining-rocm table with the ocean in the background.

The completely glass-walled dining room is connected to the pool and garden.

Full-height sliding doors activated by an electrical shaft mechanism.

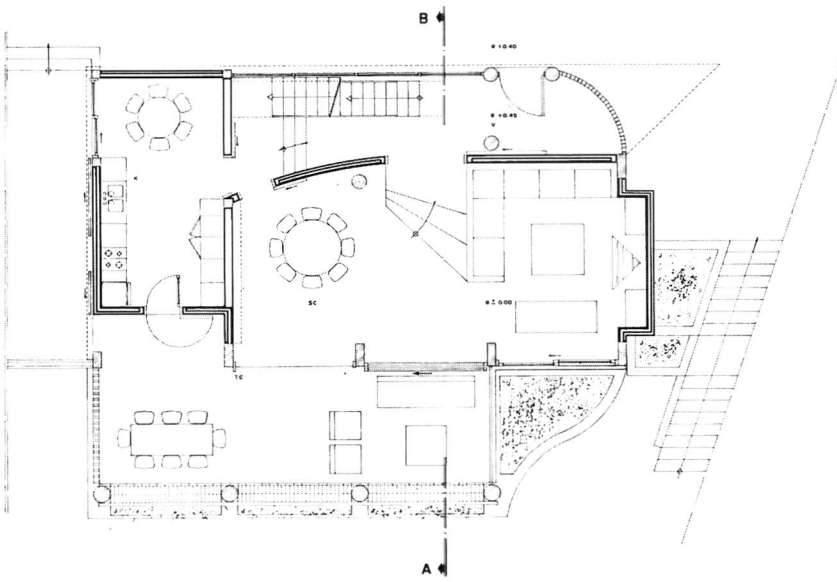

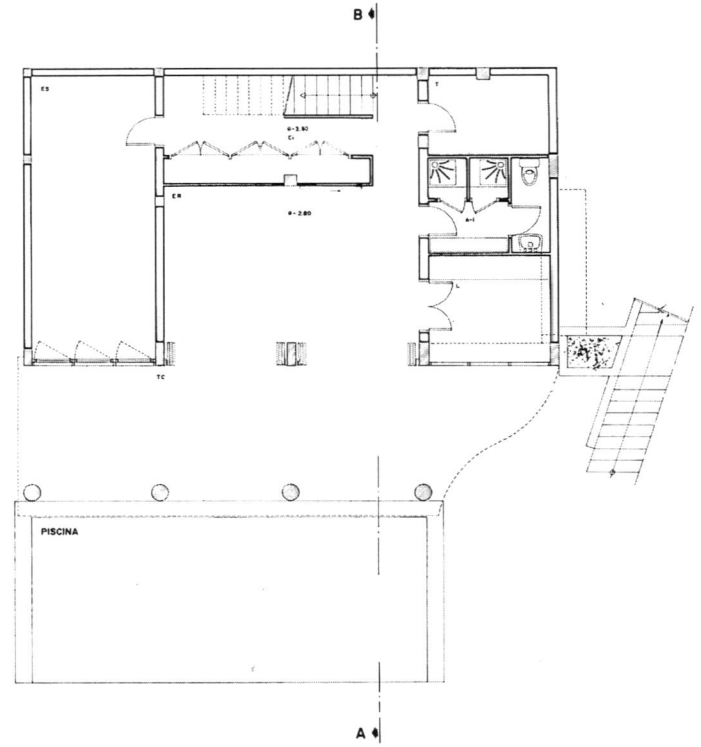

PISCINA

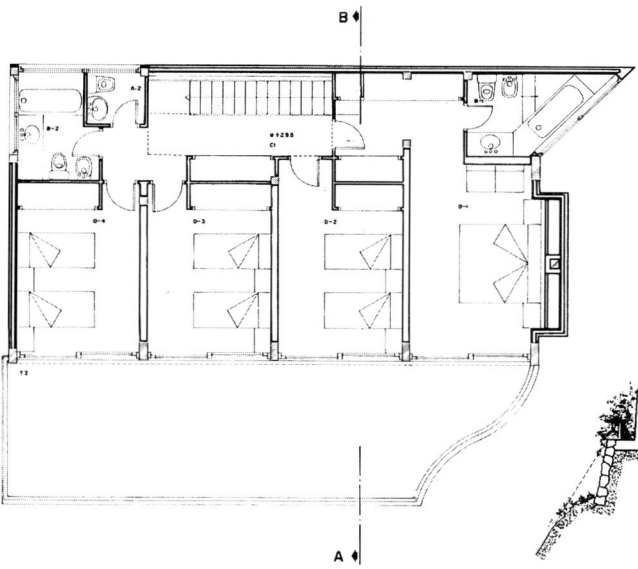

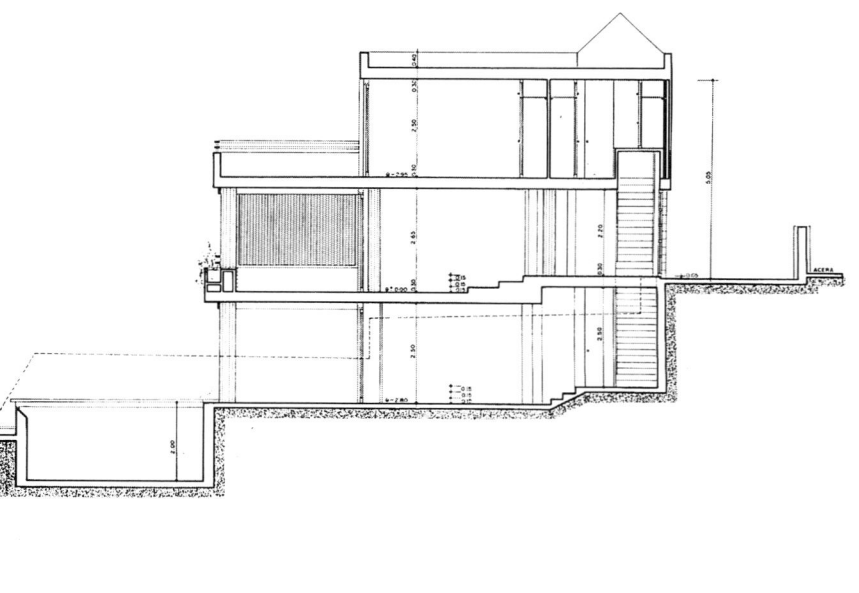

Plans of the different levels.

Section of the house.

Musical waves

Pere Nicolau

Single-family dwelling in Mallorca, Spain by Pere Nicolau.

Starting, on the one hand, from the premise of a family dwelling beside a harbour, sharing dialogue with a calm sea, and on the other hand being forced to work on a rather small site, subject to certain building restrictions imposed by the surroundings, Pere Nicolau built a dwelling which once again demonstrates what the conscience and professional attitude of a good architect can suggest as an alternative to the systematic destruction of this coastline.

This single-family dwelling is located opposite Port d'Andraitx on the devastatingly beautiful island of Mallorca, Spain, washed by the calm waters of the Mediterranean, on a site strewn with pine trees and on a sharp incline. The house has been inserted into the landscape with all due care and respect, and has been adapted to the topographical features of its privileged vantage point.

Pere Nicolau was born in 1948. He studied architecture in Barcelona's Escuela Técnica Superior de Arquitectura, and graduated with honours in 1971; he subsequently began his free-lance career. In 1976 he succesfully passed exams which gave him a place on the Ministry of Housing's official team of architects. He has been an adviser to the Balearic Islands's Town Planning Commission, technical director, a contributor to the Provincial Town Planning Commission of the Autonomous Community of the Balearic Islands from 1976 to 1984, and since then has gone on to greater things. Among his best known constructions are the project for the new terminal building and access routes to Palma airport, in partnership with two other companies, INITEC and 3T; the remodelling of the Sagrera promenade which, along with the Parc de la Mar (1984) and Sa Feixina Park (1987), constitutes the basis of the sea front construction of Palma's Old Quarter. He has won several prizes and his work has been published in specialist magazines such as Architecture d'Aujourd'hui *(Paris),* Ville Giardini Interni *and* Architectural Digest.

On a slightly irregular ground plan on one of its facades, with the task of building a normal family dwelling seeking considerable dialogue with its nautical surroundings, the architect decided to build the structure

on three levels, two at street level and one below it. These levels define the framework of the various household activities.

The floor at street level, or access floor, contains the rooms, earmarked for family life – the large living room, the dining room, the kitchen and a symmetrical arrangement on the terrace/porch. The floor above includes the evening area, including four double bedrooms and bathrooms. All these rooms open out onto a large uncovered terrace. The floor below street level opens out onto the sea, and contains those areas set aside for sport and recreation: a swimming pool, changing rooms and adjacent areas.

This building by Pere Nicolau is oriented towards the

The rectangular swimming pool extends to the very edge of the construction.

Detail of the lateral facade where the white of the walls contrasts with the green of the pine.

The house is built of common materials, and the exposed stone seen at the bottom is combined with white in the upper section.

The house is built of common materials, and the exposed stone seen at the bottom is combined with white in the upper section.

sea, the ideal architectural arrangement, and for this reason the main or access facade is a closed construction which jealously guards the privacy of the occupants and avoids unnecessary contact with the exterior. The sea elevation opposite was built in open and extrovert contrast, with a view to dialogue. In fact, the three different levels provide three different views of the sea. The top-floor terrace, which catches the morning sun and provides a view over the pine trees, also emphasises the private nature of the bedrooms. The floor below containing the lounge and dining room looks through the pine trees, its covered terrace protecting the house from the hot midday sun and establishing a more direct form of contact with the sea. Finally, the swimming pool area provides a view from underneath the pine trees.

The surrounding greenery acts as a fundamental point of reference. The whole creates tightly woven sequences which relate each level to the sea, and not only with regard to the functions of rooms on each floor.

The swimming pool, located beside the sea and blending in perfectly with its nautical setting, is the centrepiece of this structure by Pere Nicolau. This mass of water comes right up to the construction itself and, since it has been built on a fairly high level, seems to cascade down like a waterfall into the sea. The consequent fusion is almost total; the pine trees which jut out between both masses of water constitute the only parenthesis visible from the house, and the whole effect is extremely dramatic.

One of the side facades contains a heavy pointed hinge connecting it to the main facade. This geometric

93

The pure volumes which characterise the architecture of construction do not contradict its basic commonness.

Section of the house.

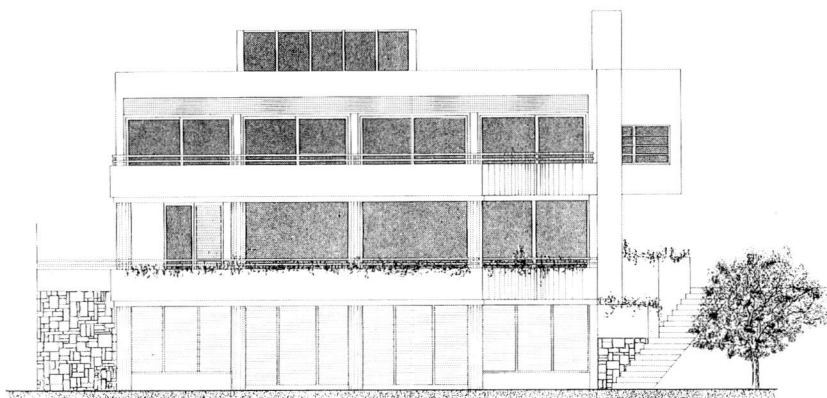

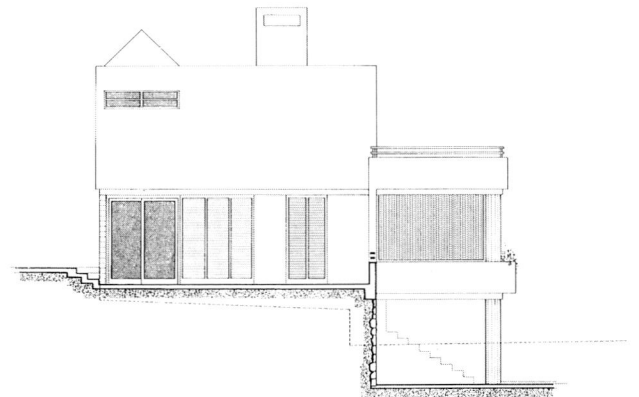

Fireplace and piano area seen from the
dining room table. The steps of the stairway
and the ceilings have a wood finish.

The furniture does not disturb the more strictly architectural richness in the least.

Perspective of the stairway with wooden steps which connects the different levels.

Interior of the kitchen with pale walls and flooring harmonising with the blue mosaic.

The modern spatial layout of the interior is functionally organised without flourishes or adornments.

View of the landscape from the covered terrace.

Section of the house.

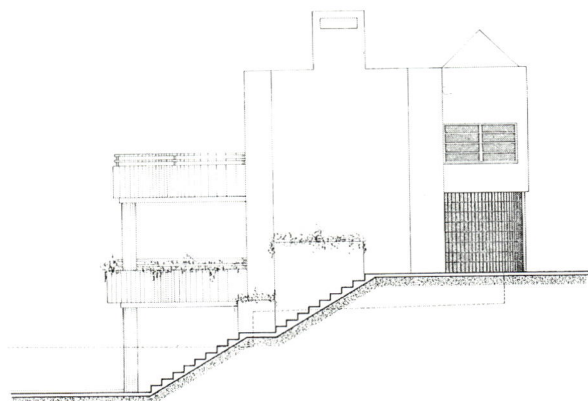

shape echoes the waves of the sea, indicating the structure's desire to blend in with the Mediterranean and creating the effect of a mobile construction. There is an additional reason for the choice of this shape: its resemblance to a grand piano does not go unnoticed – the similarly shaped piano in the lounge, for example – and the concept evokes the sound of music, a most appropriate feature from the point of view of the occupants, who take a keen interest in music. It is this very facade which houses the formal axis of the dwelling, around which the architect has laid out the various tails of this comet building.

The pure forms, which are one of the main features of this construction, relinquish none of their basic expressiveness, a normal characteristic of Pere Nicolau's

work. They rise up in all their artificial glory between the pine trees in defiance of the deep green cypress trees which, like the structure itself, reach towards the sky in striking colour contrast with their surroundings.

To solve the problem of excess sunlight caused by the fine weather so typical of this location, light passes through a skylight and indirectly through the porch and terraces. The blinds and shutters also help to reduce its strength.

The arrangement of the various areas inside the dwelling has been designed along modern lines, and responds to needs free from Baroque connotations, eliminating any potentially anecdotal features.

The house has been built from normal everyday materials; the open stonework of the outside walls'

View of the swimming pool, which seen from above seems to fall towards the sea in the background like a waterfall.

starting points combines with the white upper section, and blossoms out like a flower. The white of stainless steel door frames and windows is a constant feature, also found on the bars of the windows and on the skylight. At the entrance we find as part of the circle the rounded glass wall, which provides additional space for manoeuvring vehicles and highlights the relationship between the street elevation, the pointed hinge and the seaward facade. This entrance is lit up at night and also provides light for the garden area – during the day it provides sufficient diffused light inside the house to appreciate the sculpture by Enrique Broglia which graces this simple yet suggestive entry hall.

The interior features wood on the tread of the staircase, on the doors, ceilings, window frames and elsewhere. The simple furniture is certainly not profuse, and never disturbs the no-nonsense architectural richness – rather, it blends in beautifully with the whole.

Through his skilful combination of the deep green of the pine, the clear sharp white of the building itself and the splendid fusion of the different shades of blue in sea, sky and swimming pool, Pere Nicolau has constructed a dwelling in direct competition with the surrounding landscape, attempting dialogue with it but refusing to relinquish its own graceful air, a feature typical of most of these structures built beside the Mediterranean.

101

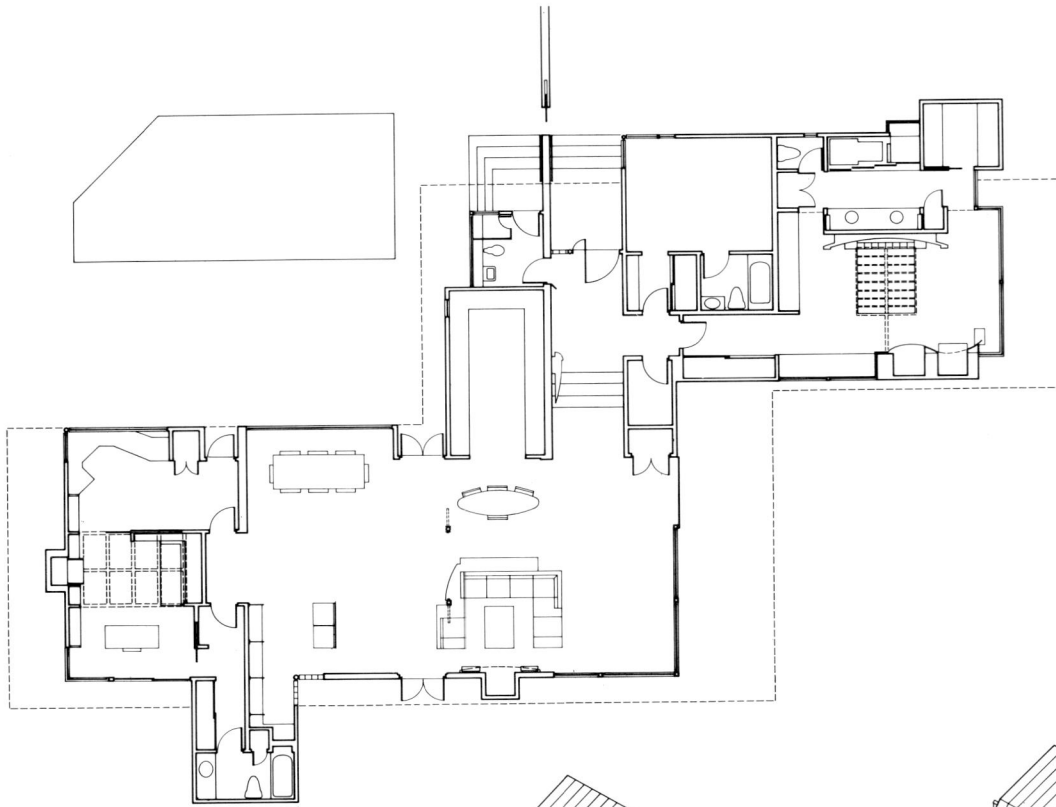

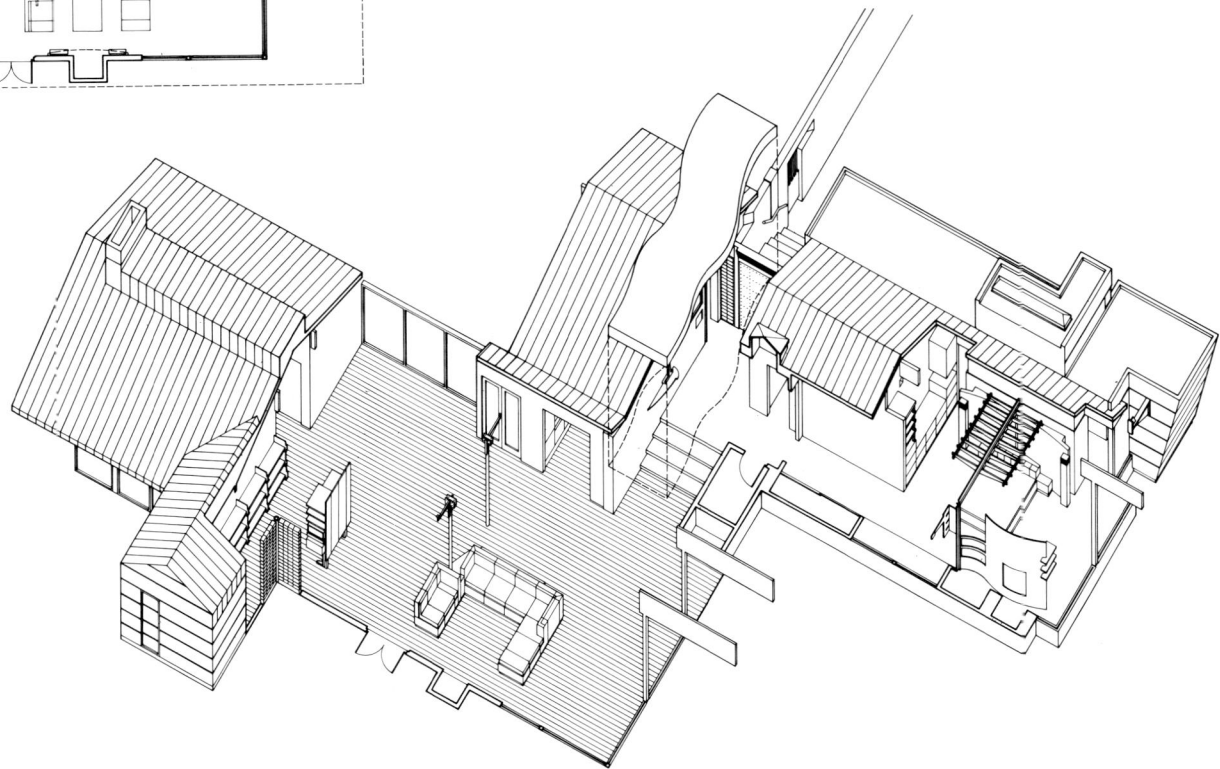

Colour contrast

Franklin D. Israel

The Arango-Berry house, situated in Beverly Hills, is a unique example of the southern California building style which has become an international legend. Franklin D. Israel is one of the architects who has made some of the most significant contributions to the contemporary image of this desirable area in California. The architect influenced by this Mediterranean heritage, has attempted to ilustrate the inherent contrasts of modern life in the city of Los Angeles. Through his work in New York and London designing schools, private houses and public buildings, he has developed a special sensitivity to differentiation and pluralism. The growth of southern California is reminiscent of a similar real-estate boom in New York in the early twentieth century. The structure of the buildings in Beverly Hills – the skyline – has introduced ritual forms, but on a smaller scale than that of the New York skycrapers.

Franklin D. Israel was born in New York in 1945 and studied architecture from 1963 to 1967 at the Philadelphia College of Arts and Sciences of the University of Pennsylvania. In 1975 he obtained a doctorate at Columbia University, New York. Before founding his own firm, he was associated with various architecture studios. Among the most prominent were Giovanni Pasanella in New York, Llewellyn Davies, Weeks, Forestier-Walker in London and Teheran, Sartoga Associates in Rome, and the Urban Design Group in New York. Among his many professional activities, his position as art director at Paramount Pictures is worthy of note. In 1983 he set up his own studio where he has executed numerous

One of the two large rectangular parallelepipeds by the house.

The simple metal entrance gate is set into
the blue wall.

Detail of the roof, the terrace and the original swimming pool.

Section of the main facade.

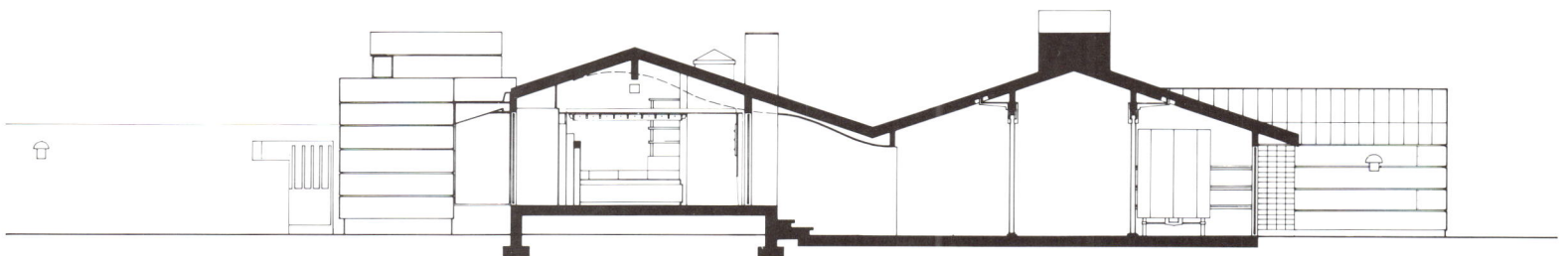

The blue of the exterior is repeated in the entrance gallery which leads to the living room.

Original piece of furniture used for storing records. Abstract painting in the foreground.

important projects: the remodelling of Propaganda Film Studios (Hollywood), Klein House (Bel Air, California), Arango-Berry House (Los Angeles, California), a residence in Semel Beach (Malibu, California), the Honey Springs Country Club (San Diego, California), the Houseman (Brentwood, California), and offices for the Mathematical Applications Group, Inc. (Santa Monica, California).

Franklin D. Israel has received several awards for his professional work and has participated as a visiting professor in lectures on urban planning and architecture for university students. In 1987 he established the Los Angeles Forum for Architecture and Urban Design. His work has appeared in Vogue, The Architectural Digest, The New York Times, and many other newspapers and professional magazines.

This project was based on an original structure built in 1950, which was almost in ruins. The state of deterioration of the building made it necessary to demolish the old external wall and construct new ones. The house, owned by a scriptwriter/producer, was enlarged and completely remodelled.

When this process was completed, the structure consisted of two rectangles joined on one of their two longer sides. The enlargement was introduced in the rectangle opposite the module containing the main entrance, and consisted basically of adding a bathroom and dressing rooms. These, like the roof, were constructed in galvanised metal sheeting. The extension and remodelling resulted in a spacious building formed by two rectangular parallelepipeds. These two constructions share a single vast roof where the heating and air conditioning systems and the ventilation ducts have been concealed.

The main entrance to the residence is set into the blue opaque stucco wall which encloses the garden. This new structural element is in tune with Israel's creative spirit. He has an affinity for the interplay of contrasting colours, always opting for fresh and surprising combinations. The opening in the wall which constitues the entrance is in the unusual shape of an inverted L. It is closed by a black iron gate remarkable for the simplicity of its design.

Israel left the existing swimming pool intact, but extended the brick wall which surrounds it to meet the blue stuccoed concrete wall of the garden. This blue wall is one of the dominating elements in the exterior design. The architect extended the wall horizontally to create a link between the new garage and the main entrance and to flank the entry gallery as far as the living room, thus penetrating the interior space.

The house is on one floor, but there are interior differences in level which are spanned by short flights of steps. At the level of the entry gallery and opening off it is the door to the bedrooms and their adjoining bathrooms. At the end of the corridor, which has an original undulating ceiling, the visitor reaches the kitchen and the living room/dining room. The large, unobstructed spaces are impressive, and the natural light lends the

The bed in the master bedroom is made of glossy steel. The natural light shining in through the floor-to-ceiling window fills the room.

The geometric rug in shades of blue defines the path to be taken.

Panoramic view of the living room.

rooms a pleasant transparency. The main bathroom and the dressing rooms added by Israel can be reached from this section.

The original layout, designed in the fifties, was retained. Large windows and walls of glass and concrete afford new perspectives of the city. Access to the interior of the house is through a swing door, which pivots on a central bolt and has a steel and glass lintel. The entry gallery which begins at this point is covered by a curvilinear plaster ceiling. This rather dark corridor is countered by the brightness of the living room/dining room to which it leads. The natural light which floods the room is filtered through the glass walls which enclose it.

The entire interior of the house has been redecorated. The cabinet containing the television set and the hi-fi

equipment, the fireplace and the bed in the master bedroom are all built-in structures finished in glossy steel.

F. D. Israel's architecture reflects his ambition to express fresh and singular ideas in each one of his projects.

In remodelling and enlarging the Arango-Berry House, he used common, conventional materials like concrete, steel, stucco, plaster and brick.

He has created an eclectic and unique design, accentuating the aesthetic aspect. The colour contrast in the facàdes of whites and greys, with a contrasting note provided by the blue walls, is repeated in the interior in the white walls, the glossy steel of the smaller structures (the fireplace, the bed and the cabinet for the hi-fi equipment) and the blue rug in the living room. Through

The carved wooden ornamentation symbol-
ises welcome.

Detail of the living room.

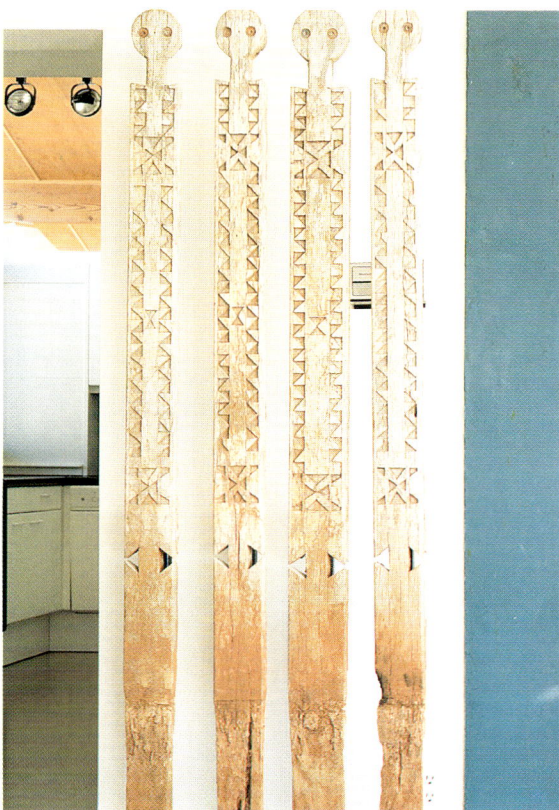

these colour schemes and the interplay of straight lines
and curves, the architect has created a lively visual effect,
a certain intensity, and subtle variations in the surfaces,
maintaining a dialogue with the surroundings, as well as
between the external and internal configuration of the
dwelling itself.

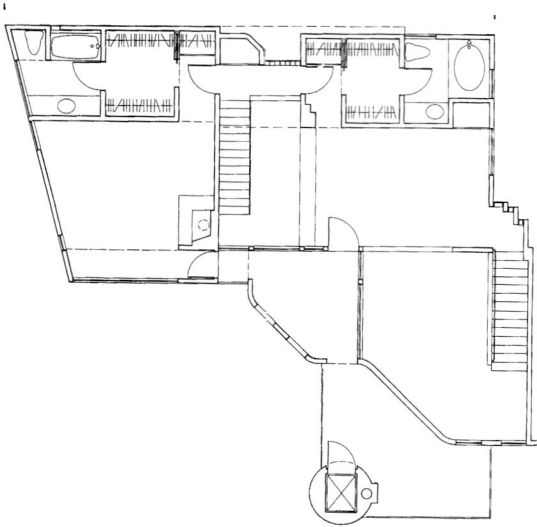

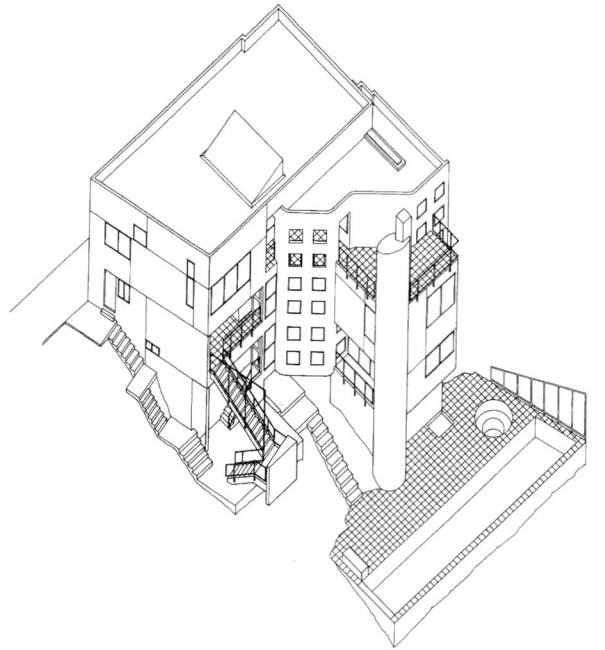

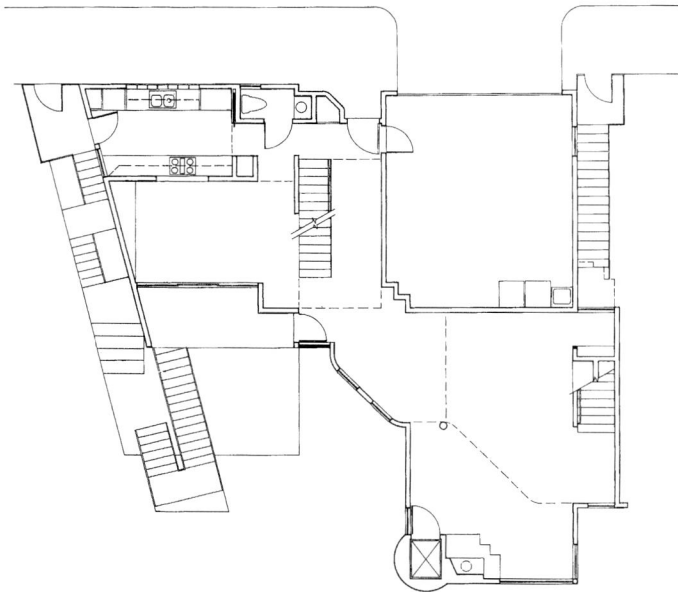

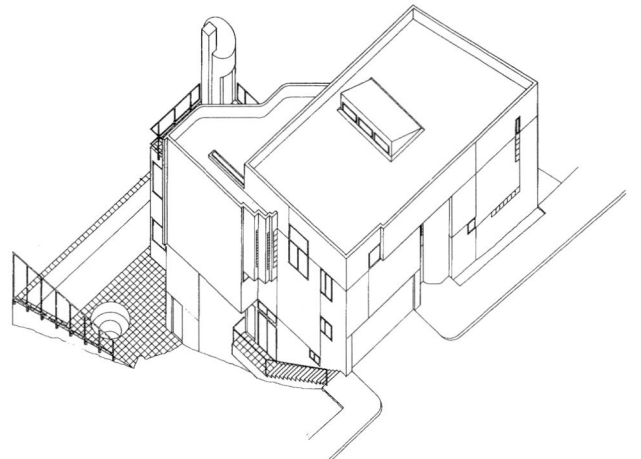

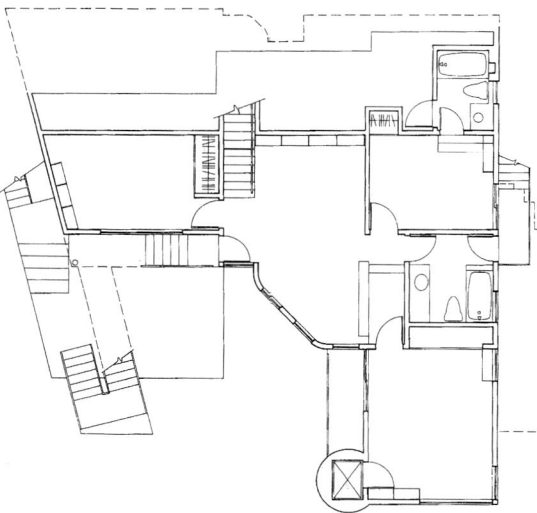

Upper level.

Middle level.

Lower level.

Isometry of the south elevation.

Isometry of the north elevation.

Angular forms and planes

J. Frank Fitzgibbons

Built on a site in a residential zone in Los Angeles, California, Irmala House is in a privileged location offering magnificent views which stretch from the east with the metropolis at its feet, right across to Santa Monica in the west, and to the ocean in the distance. The entire interior of the house enjoys the excellent advantages of its southern aspect and the vistas of the surrounding landscape.

J. Frank Fitzgibbons, the architect responsible for the project, studied architecture at the University of Michigan and has worked for several studios in New York, Bern and Rome. He has lived in California since 1977 finally settling in Los Angeles. He set up his own private studio of architecture and sculpture in 1985, working on both commercial premises and private residences. His

sculpture has been exhibited on various occasions, such as the exhibition at the Pacific Design Centre of Los Angeles. He is a member of the American Institute of Architects, and president of the Architectural Foundation of Los Angeles. His projects have been published in numerous specialised architectural journals such as Toshu-Jutaku (Japan, 1986), L.A. Style (USA, 1987, 1988), Interior Design (USA, 1989), World Residential Design 07 (USA, 1990).

Fitzgibbons' plans for this project were extremely complex; involving the renovation of a building consisting of two apartments, both duplexes. He extended the building by approximately 1,000 square feet combining the two areas into a homogeneous whole. Previously there had been no internal connection between the two apartments.

111

The angular forms and straight lines which
define the exterior are repeated inside the
house.

When the conversion was completed, the
construction appeared from the outside to be a single
two-storey block. As one goes down the hill on which the
building is sited, however, one can gradually discern the
four storeys of which it in fact consists, plus a terrace
with swimming pool. The overall impression is of a
compact rectangle with indications of movement, an
effect caused by the inclination of the site. Fitzgibbons
has achieved a biform building which, on the north-facing
side, is dominated by simple straight lines, while the rear
facade is governed by more complex forms which are
reflected in the interior of the house.

The different floors are linked by short flights of steps
which connect the top terrace to the swimming pool
level. The form therefore seems to be set afloat from the

main mass of the building in order to define the plane of
the eastern facade. The southern elevation follows the
contours of the site at a ten-degree angle, flattening out
where it merges with the level of the swimming pool.

The plane formed by the main facade is repeated on
the eastern facade, but in the form of a projecting beam.
The pattern of the coloured curved plane is picked up
again as a jutting wall behind the projecting element, and
this bends, wrapping itself around the exterior south-
facing wall in a complex curve, and merges into the first
section of the house. It later reoccurs in the L shape
formed by the lower mass which extends out southwards
towards the city.

The entrance to the house consists of a large volume
which takes up two floors and is made to look narrower

Detail of the north facade, showing the circular sky-blue structure.

The rear elevation is composed of complex forms which are reproduced inside the house; at the end, the tube containing the lift.

On the southern facade, the rows of small, square windows provide ample natural light.

Interior of the living room.

by the curved plane of bright steel on the roof. The undulating glossy surface of this element contrasts with the white sand walls. Square windows are dotted along the entire length of the wall in vertical and horizontal lines, dividing the facade visually into smaller planes as if it were a block of buildings or lines connecting the doors and windows.

As mentioned above the building is divided into four floors to take advantage of the steep slope of the site. The house includes a two-car garage, kitchen, dining room, living room, three bedrooms, two studies, a library, four bathrooms and a sauna on the lower floor. Excluding the garage, the house has a surface area of approximately 3,100 square feet. The reception rooms are located at street level, while the upper and lower

floors are reserved for more private rooms. The architect has created a very open construction by providing each floor with exterior terraces.

The interior spaces are connected horizontally and vertically. The height of the ceilings varies considerably from 7 to 24 feet. The angular forms and straight lines which define the building on the exterior are repeated inside, including a complex curved wall which modifies the curved plane of the ceiling in the entrance hall; it is made of handworked copper, moulded into undulating forms to reflect the natural light filtering in through the clear glass skylight and spreading a warm rosy glow when reflected by the copper.

The swimming pool, jacuzzi, sauna, lift, cellar and storage space, a machine room and a terrace are all

Designer chair on a tiled floor.

The fireplace and windows in one of the bedrooms.

located on the lowest floor. The second floor is made up of an office, two bathrooms, two bedrooms, a terrace and the library. The entrance to the house is located on the third floor, which houses the dining room, the garage, a small laundry room, a balcony, the living room, the kitchen and a small washroom. The top floor has two large bathrooms, a double bedroom, a study, a covered gallery and a terrace which is used as a solarium.

The lift is installed in a circular tower situated on the ocean-facing facade, covered in galvanised laminated metal. This tower also houses part of the chimney, which appears on the outside as a red square block contrasting with the cylindrical block containing the lift in a play on angular forms and colour. The floor of the lift slopes in the direction of the house thus exaggerating its rounded form.

The same pale yellow metal tubing and metallic mesh used for the safety banisters and railings is employed both inside and outside the house. Outside, the floors are finished with oak planking, while the interior is tiled throughout. The interior walls are all white, the curved copper piece providing the only colour contrast.

Fitzgibbons has used straight and angular lines to delimit the planes in this design, where the windows filtering the light play an extremely important role. Both inside and out, the separate volumes come together to establish a dialogue. The forms are repeated on various scales and in modified ways, making the construction conform to a series of details which fuse into a homogeneous whole.

Detail of the southern facade.

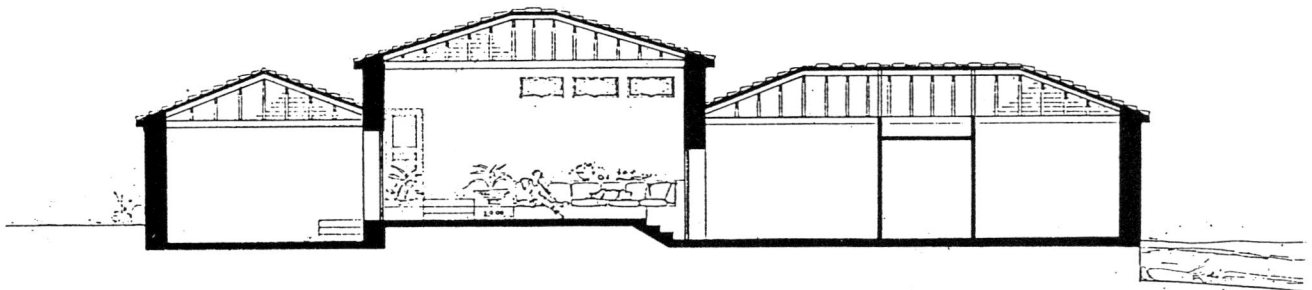

Architecture by units

Michel Photiadis

House in Kouzono Bay, on the island of Spetsai, Greece by Michel Photiadis.

Located in Kouzono Bay, on the Greek island of Spetsai, this house was built on flat terrain on an 8,000-m² site surrounded by olive trees, between road and sea. The front of the house and its sides face the coast. Plans for the construction of the volume were made with Spetsai's standards and regulations very much in mind – the dwelling had to be built in such a way as to respect the architectural style of the island, and was not to cover an area greater than 200 m².

The Athens architect Michel Photiadis was in charge of this construction. Having studied in the United States, in 1965 he founded the company M. Photiadis Architectes Associés. Among his architectural achievements in Greece are: the Athens Prison, the Great Britain Hotel in Athens, the American College of Greece in Pierce, the Tsitouras Foundation, the Santorini Museum on the island of the same name and the Katranzos sport department store chain in Athens, Thessalonika and Herakleion. He has lectured in architecture and has written on the subject in magazines published in Greece and abroad. He has lectured in architecture and has written on the subject in magazines published in Greece and abroad. He has been awarded several prizes – from the Corfu Ionian Academy for his renovation work on the Greek Centre of European Studies, and from the Greek Ministry of Housing for the traditional Greek houses built by him in Patmos, Corfu and Spetsai.

The vibrant blue French windows of the lounge lead directly onto the whitewashed terrace.

The large terrace is arranged on two levels and this separation is achieved by two steps.

Construction work was carried out on four units, all topped by a four-sided roof. These four blocks mark out the building from inside and outside. In order to comply with building restrictions regarding the surface area, the house has been enlarged by outdoor units, each one of which is an elongation of the interior structure.

The front of the house faces the sea, and this facade is the location for the three entrance doors and a large split-level terrace. Three of the four units can be seen from this elevation: the central unit, with its wood and glass doors painted blue; and two side units which border the large terrace – the bedrooms are located within these units. The two levels of the terrace are separated by two white steps which add a splendid brightness to the structure. The materials used were extremely simple

rough-cut square beams for the basic shell, old-fashioned tiling on the roofs and lightly coloured terrace tiling.

From the back elevation, which provides access to the house, all four blocks can be seen, the central unit rising above the other three to articulate and centre the whole building. Points of interest regarding the entrance patio are round-edged mosaics, typical of the island, forming a square within the light tiling, and a small water trough built on the white floor, all of which lend the patio an unmistakeable touch of beauty and taste. On this facade there is also the occasional flower motif sculpture, a design also very typical of this region. The kitchen patio can be used as an open-air dining room and includes a covering of rushes arranged over wooden beams as protection from the hot Greek sun.

Thanks to the skilful work of the architect, the carpenter and also to the island's other craftsmen, this building was finished in seven months. The outside walls, 40 cm. thick, are insulated by material under pressure and include guttering which guides rainwater into a 150-m^3 tank below the main terrace. In this way, these four blocks which make up the dwelling's basic layout endow it with strength and beauty, and also determine the internal arrangement and the location of the different rooms.

The patio with the round-edged mosaics leads to the front door of the house in the main unit, and here we find the hall and a large lounge-cum-dining room, with certain zones clearly marked out by means of a white fireplace, which stretches from the ochre tiling up to the roof, a construction of superimposed wooden beams. The lounge leads through to the large outside terrace facing the sea, and is separated from the terrace by the three doors made of glass and blue wood. This room also receives exterior light via an open skylight – the light even reaches one of the walls. Most of the furniture – in this room, the sofas, the shelving and the tables – has been incorporated into the structure of the building; in other words, they have been embedded into the walls. The owner of the house has a habitable construction, ready for use, since the decor has been built into the basic structure itself. The dining room table is an extremely original design – brown tiles with a large flower pattern.

The entrance patio displays a square stone mosaic, in the form of a star surrounded by light floor tiling.

121

Most of the furniture is built into the
construction, for example the chimney in the
spacious lounge.

Plan of the ground floor.

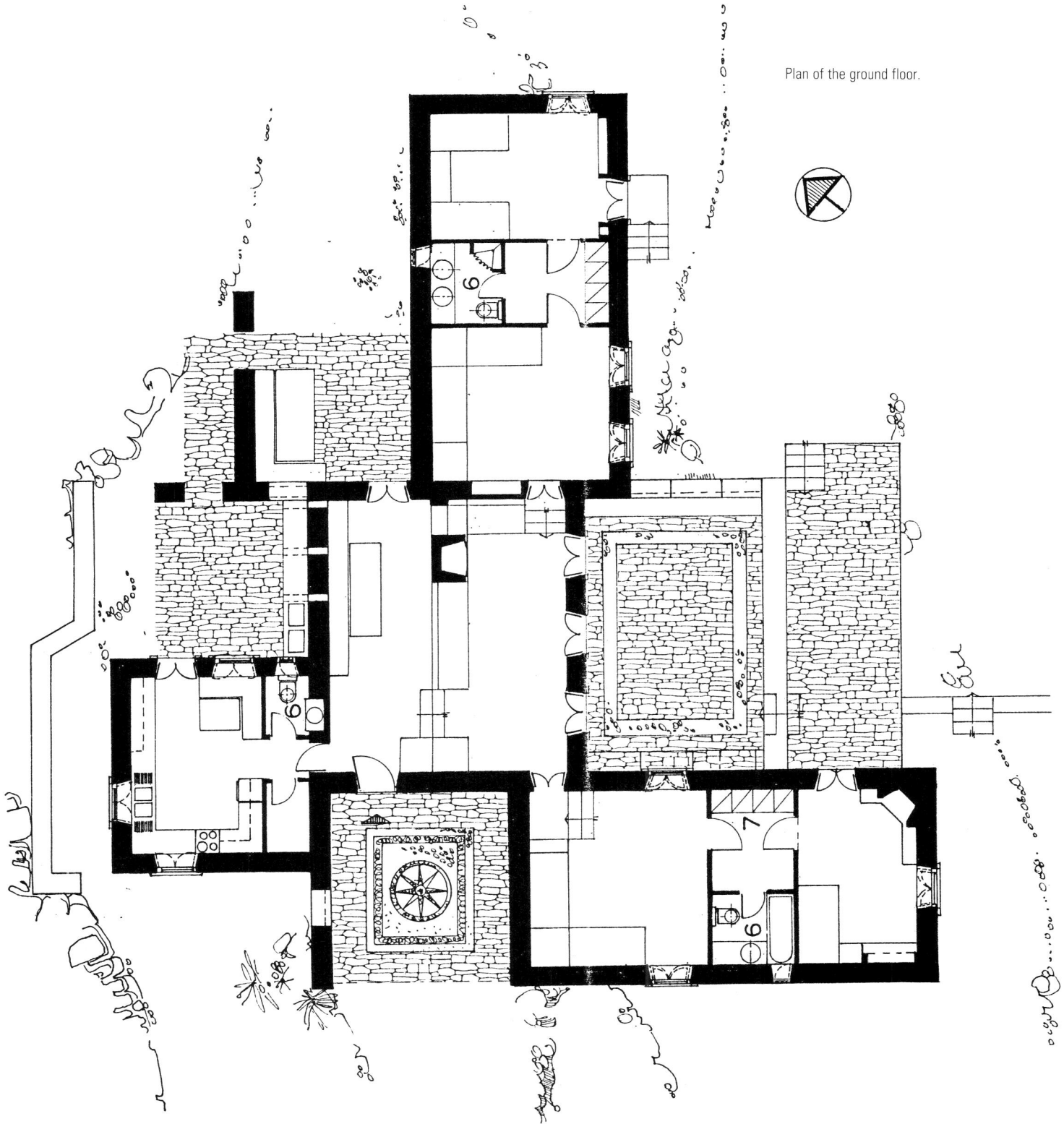

White walls and light paving in one of the
bedrooms.

Blue woodwork and white walls in another
of the rooms.

Behind this main unit is the block housing the kitchen, cloakroom and a bathroom. The kitchen extension is a patio which serves as a summer dining room, with similar features to the other external facilities.

The main block is likewise flanked by two more which contain the bedrooms. The block to the right has a horizontal projection and contains two rooms separated by a bathroom. These rooms boast the same decor as the lounge/dining room: the beds have been built into the structure of the building, as has the bedside table. All the walls are white, the tiling is ochre cement and the ceiling has been constructed using reinforced wooden beams.

The block to the left, however, projects along the vertical; it is an extension of the entrance patio and abuts lengthways with the terrace overlooking the sea. Here we

find two more rooms, also separated by a bathroom, and with the same decor as the other two; furniture built into the architectural structure and wooden ceilings contrasting with the white of the walls and the blue woodwork. A wooden door opens into the bathroom, and here the interior design makes a break with the other rooms in the house – it is not white, but rather the same ochre as the cement floor, finished with a wooden ceiling in the same colour.

In short, this dwelling on the Greek island of Spetsai is structured into four distinct blocks which successfully distribute interior and exterior space. The construction brings strength and originality to the whole, whose interior decoration is built into the architectural structure itself for practical and also aesthetic reasons. Equally, it

The lounge, with its ochre floor paving and wooden moss beams, is separated from the terrace by the blue wooden and glass doors.

View of the dining room: the brown tiles of the table with large floral design in the foreground.

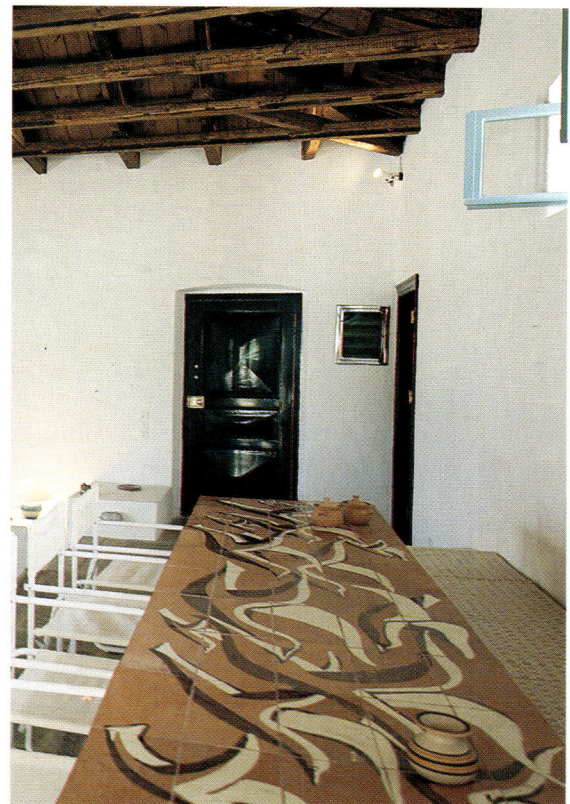

has been built in strict adherence to the island's rules and regulations. It has several splendid decorative features, charactristic of this corner of the Mediterranean – the round-edged mosaics in the entrance patio and the wall sculptures – all of which are enhanced by natural light from the windows and external patios, a picture framed by this incomparable Greek landscape.

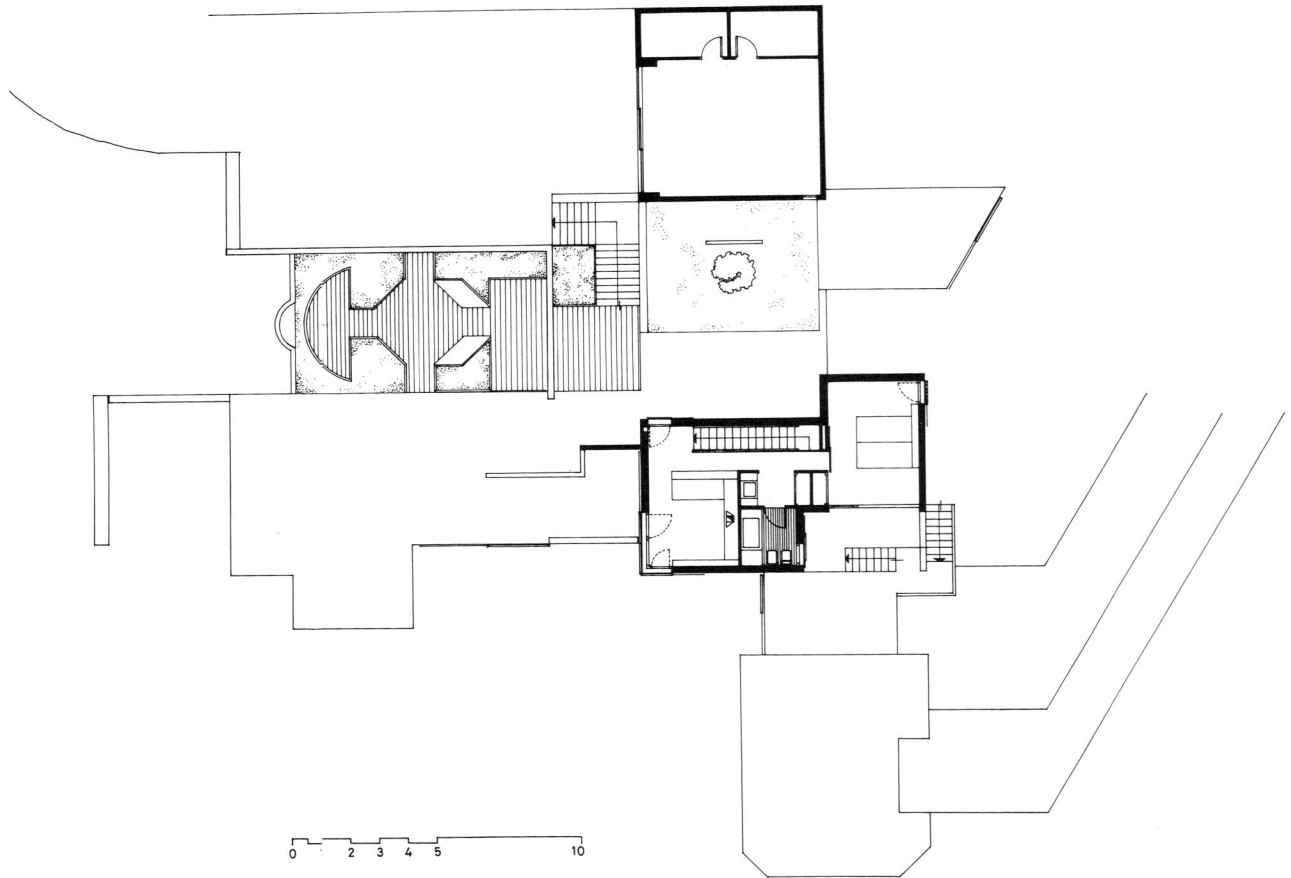

0 2 3 4 5   10

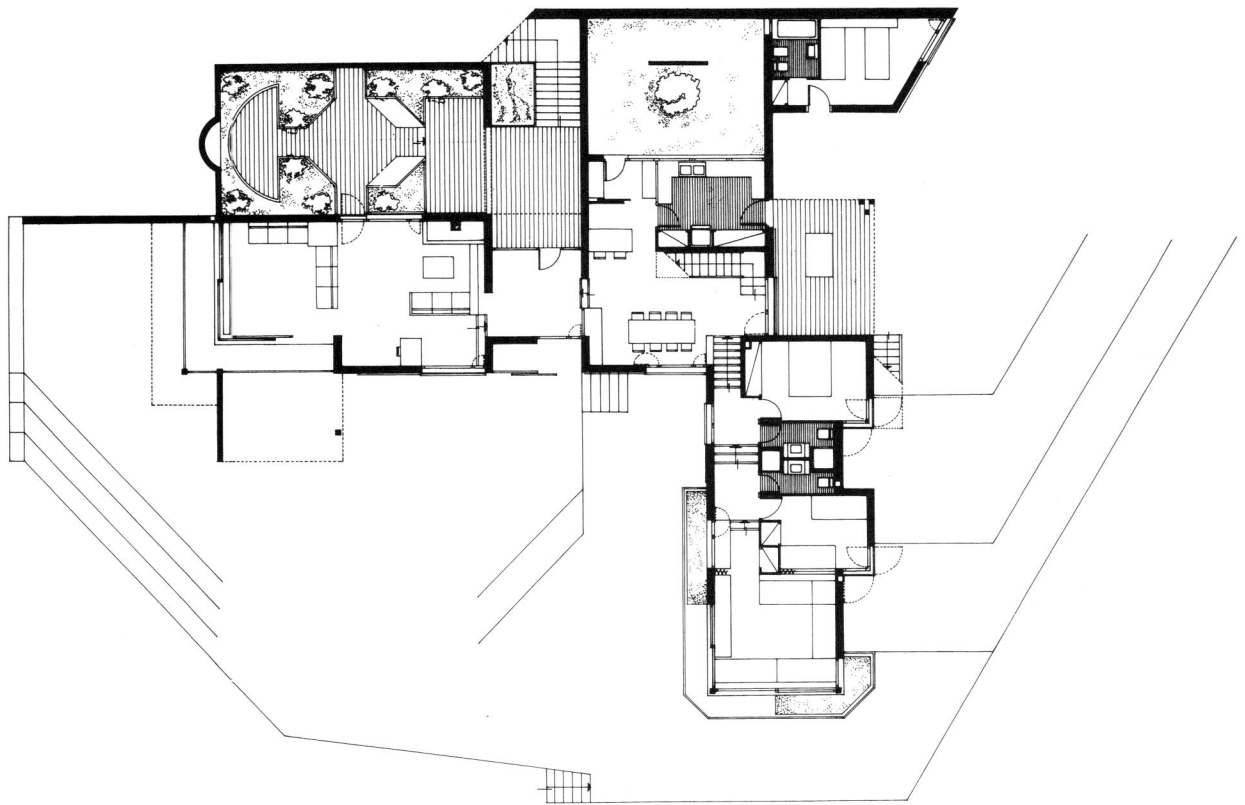

White textured cubes

Víctor Rahola

Single-family dwelling on the Costa Brava, Girona (Spain) by Víctor Rahola.

This house was built at a picturesque location on the Costa Brava by Víctor Rahola. Its reluctance to open up without further ado toward the splendour of the nearby sea, a typical trait of houses built along the coastline opposite geographical features of such inherent beauty and power, means that the various parts of the building turn in towards the centre of the structure itself in a bid for independence and autonomy.

This single-family dwelling is located at the very heart of the Costa Brava in Girona province, Spain. More specifically, it is situated on Cap Norfeu, an area within the Roses district. It was built on a sharply sloping hillside projecting into the sea, and the structure has adapted to this site with the greatest of ease. The surrounding terrain is slightly irregular and strewn with rocks; the vegetation consists mainly of olive trees and scrub. This privileged vantage point provides fantastic views of the sea and the rough untamed coves so typical of the Mediterranean coastline.

Víctor Rahola was born in Barcelona in 1945. He studied architecture there at the Escuela Técnica Superior de Arquitectura, and worked for two years in J. A. Coderch's studio, submitting his end-of-course design in 1973. That same year he opened a studio in Barcelona in partnership with Salvador Soteras, an architect and stress engineer. Since 1977 he has lectured on Projects II in the Escuela Técnica Superior de Arquitectura in Barcelona. His design was the prizewinner

Sections of the house.

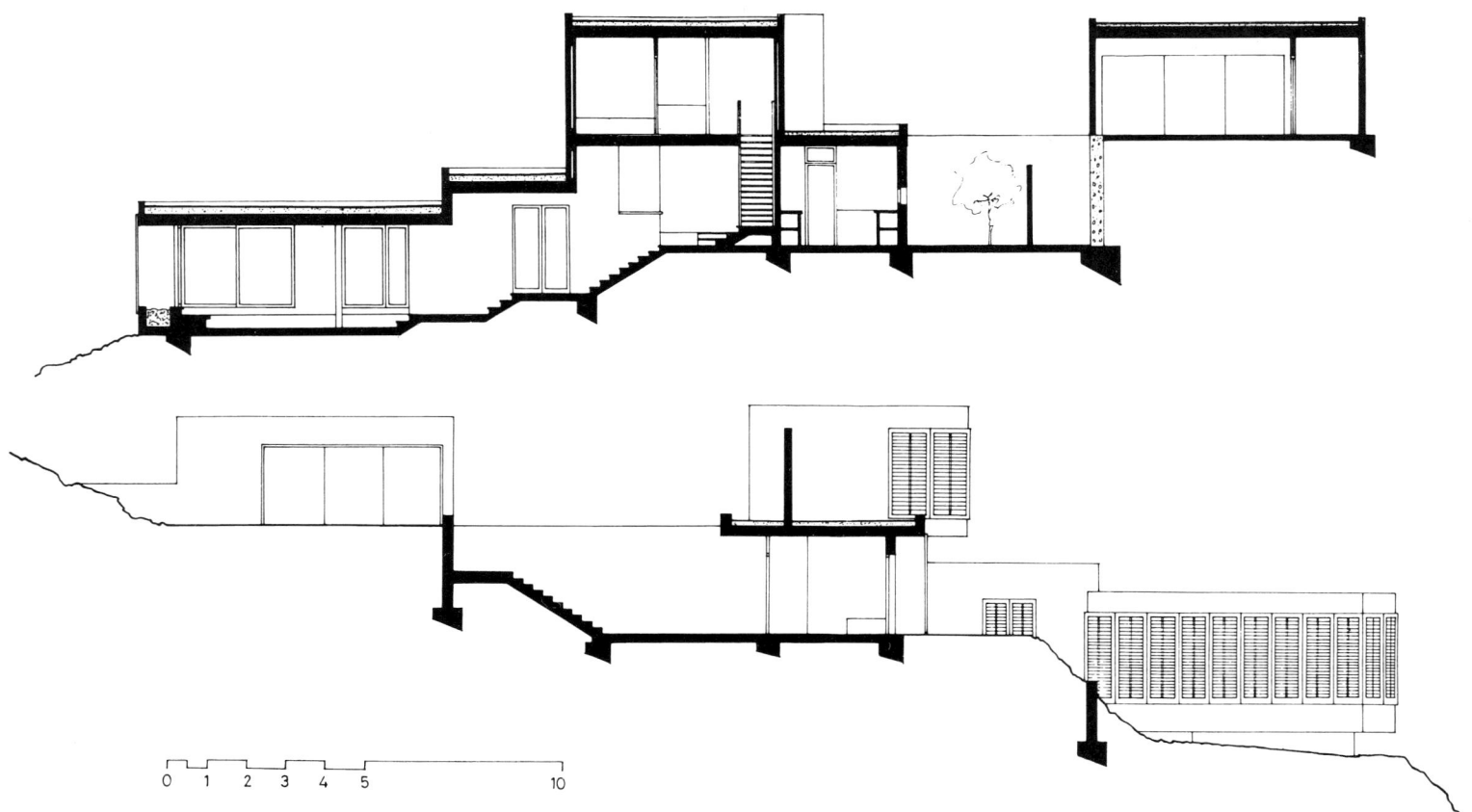

```
0   1   2   3   4   5           10
```

in the 1985 FAD architectural competition, runner-up in Palma de Mallorca's competition for the design of exhibition and conference halls in 1989, nominated again for the 1989 and 1990 FAD prizes and jury's choice for the 1990 Miës van der Rohe prize. This architect has published several articles on his work in magazines such as El Croquis, Quaderns, On and Diario de Mallorca. His most outstanding constructions are a technical school in Cambrils, a four-star hotel on the island of Ibiza (1988), design and construction of a square in the city of Barcelona (1989), Girona's Official School of Languages, the Telecommunications Faculty of the Universitat Politècnica de Catalunya (1990), several secondary schools and also many single-family dwellings, such as this construction on the Costa Brava.

This structure, built on an irregular ground plan, consists of tiered units in the shape of an L. One block with a large door contains the garage; beside this there is a staircase which descends at an angle towards a doorway, which in turn leads into a secluded geometric garden at the side. The hall/entrance area divides the family area from the rest of the dwelling; the dining room, breakfast bar and kitchen have been laid out along the same building line, whilst all the bedrooms are located in a block situated on a lower level. From the dining room a wooden staircase leads to the area most used by the parents – a library or study, a bedroom suite with fully- equipped bathroom.

Behind the kitchen there is a patio enclosed by an olive grove, creating an open space which serves to emphasise,

128

all the more clearly, the different levels and the size of the building. On the other side of this patio there is a totally separate bedroom and bathroom for guests.

The consecutive layout of these white cubic units, and the fact that they are flanked by a series of olive groves, are the main features which depict the house as a defiant huddle, shunning the most envious of situations a stone's throw from the sea. Thus this single-family dwelling by Víctor Rahola makes good its partial escape from nautical surroundings, turning in upon itself to ensure the inclusion of the various units within the whole, asserting its intrinsic independence and worth. The hackneyed concept, however, of a Mediterranean dwelling perched at the edge of a rough and harsh coastline like some

Pyrenean Colophon, is superbly assimilated.

A series of features has been included so as to conceal the structure and mould it into the landscape. For instance, the roof is completely flat and covered with gravel chippings; the enclosing wall which marks out the boundary of the property is the same colour as the rocky scrub terrain surrounding it. Despite these hesitant and uncertain attempts the spectacular dimensions of the dwelling stand out, the brilliant white providing a vivid contrast to the other colour hues in this Mediterranean seascape painting; a clear colour distinction is defined between the blue of the sea at the front of the building and the blue of the sky overhead, and the structure is perceived as lost in a sea of greenery.

The house is constructed on an irregular base, and the volumes are laid out in a steplike manner.

129

The patios and interior gardens at the rear of
the house capture light and air.

An enclosed patio behind the kitchen
creates an empty space which emphasises
the volumetric form of the house and the
differences in levels.

*The building features many openings facing the sea,
which allow the sun to enter the dwelling and provide the
occupants with a variety of views of the surrounding
landscape. On the other hand, at the back of the house
there are very few windows – just those necessary to
ensure adequate ventilation throughout the entire house.
In fact, light is captured with great ease on this side of the
house by means of the interior gardens and patios. So as
to avoid any unpleasant excess typical of the climate of
the location, the house boasts a protective barrier of
wooden shutters which weakens the sun's rays and
reduces the strength of the north winds, the Tramontana
for instance, which vent their wrath on this coastline.*

*Inside the building there are several small corners for
rest and relaxation which enhance the concept of*

*seclusion and life behind closed doors. For this reason
the windows of the various main rooms which provide
magnificent views of the landscape once again
constitute, at the occupants' own request, a means of
establishing a direct relationship with these surroundings.*

*The gravel chippings on the roof are also used on the
interior patios, unifying the whole. The composition of the
floors is extremely varied; wood which matches most of
the furniture or the dark rustic ceramics. The walls and
ceilings are all painted white.*

*In spite of its splendid natural surroundings, this
single-family dwelling by Víctor Rahola appears to have
been designed for a life led behind closed doors; the very
vegetation, with the help of the gardens and patios
concealed behind the walls, forms part of the architectural*

View of the house set on the hillside. The retaining wall is built of materials of the same colour as the terrain.

structure. There is however, some shifting of values more attributable to hesitation or indecision on the part of the architect than to any strong beliefs held by him. This is most clearly demonstrated in the use of openings to the exterior, and by the assimilation of local colours and materials. In any case, the spectacular white dimensions of this dwelling constitute its most obvious individual feature.

The white features of the layout of this grouped series of cubic volumes can be appreciated.

The roofs of the house are totally flat, covered with gravel.

The privileged situation of the house and the large windows afford fabulous views of the sea and the wild and rustic coves.

The rear facade is more closed and compact. The facade entrance is also on this side.

Detail of the gravel-covered roofs.

The second level of the house includes a geometrically-shaped enclosed garden.

The large windows of the main rooms are oriented towards the views of the landscape.

View of the dining room, from which access is gained to the upper floor.

The fireplace area with grey tiles and white walls and kilims.

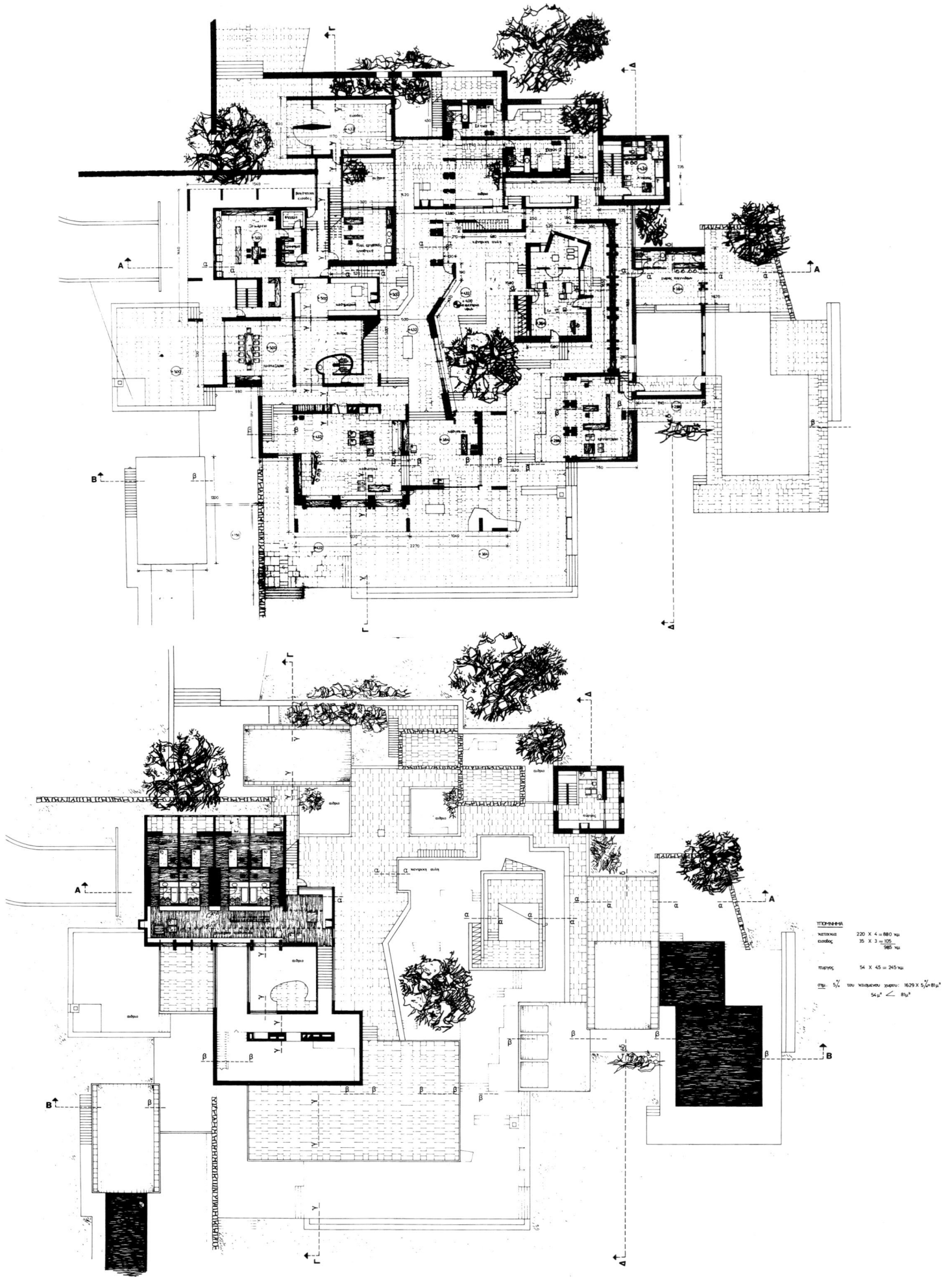

Plan of the ground floor.

Plan of the first floor.

Greek Orthodox monastery by the sea

Ilias Papayannopoulos

The Greek architect Ilias Papayannopoulos designed this house in Cassandra-Chalcidice in the historic Macedonian region of the Balkan peninsula. The plans have been exhibited in Paris, Brussels, Athens and other important Greek cities, and published in numerous specialised publications. The interest generated by this project stems from recognition of the creative work which went into the design and construction of this private residence.

Ilias Papayannopoulos (Athens, 1939) graduated in 1965 from the Technological University in Athens. During his student years, he received a grant from the Department of Art History of the University of Sienna, where he obtained the title of doctor of sciences in art history. He also studied painting and sculpture. When he completed his studies, he worked as a lecturer in the Technological University in Athens under the direction of Professor Iannis Despotopoulos (who studied at the Bauhaus in pre-Nazi Germany). Papayannopoulos has designed and built many single-family residences, public and commercial buildings, and hotels, and has also designed and implemented the interior decoration of all these buildings. He was elected vice-president of the Greek Chamber of Architects, and has received numerous awards for his work.

Macedonia has not had any particular architectural style since 1922, which was the year Greek refugees arrived there from Asia Minor. The refugees built improvised houses, designed with a view to meeting their most immediate needs. These houses do not have any

The rooms are grouped according to function, and the height of each group is different.

The brick walls of the house were plastered and then whitewashed.

Different sections of the house.

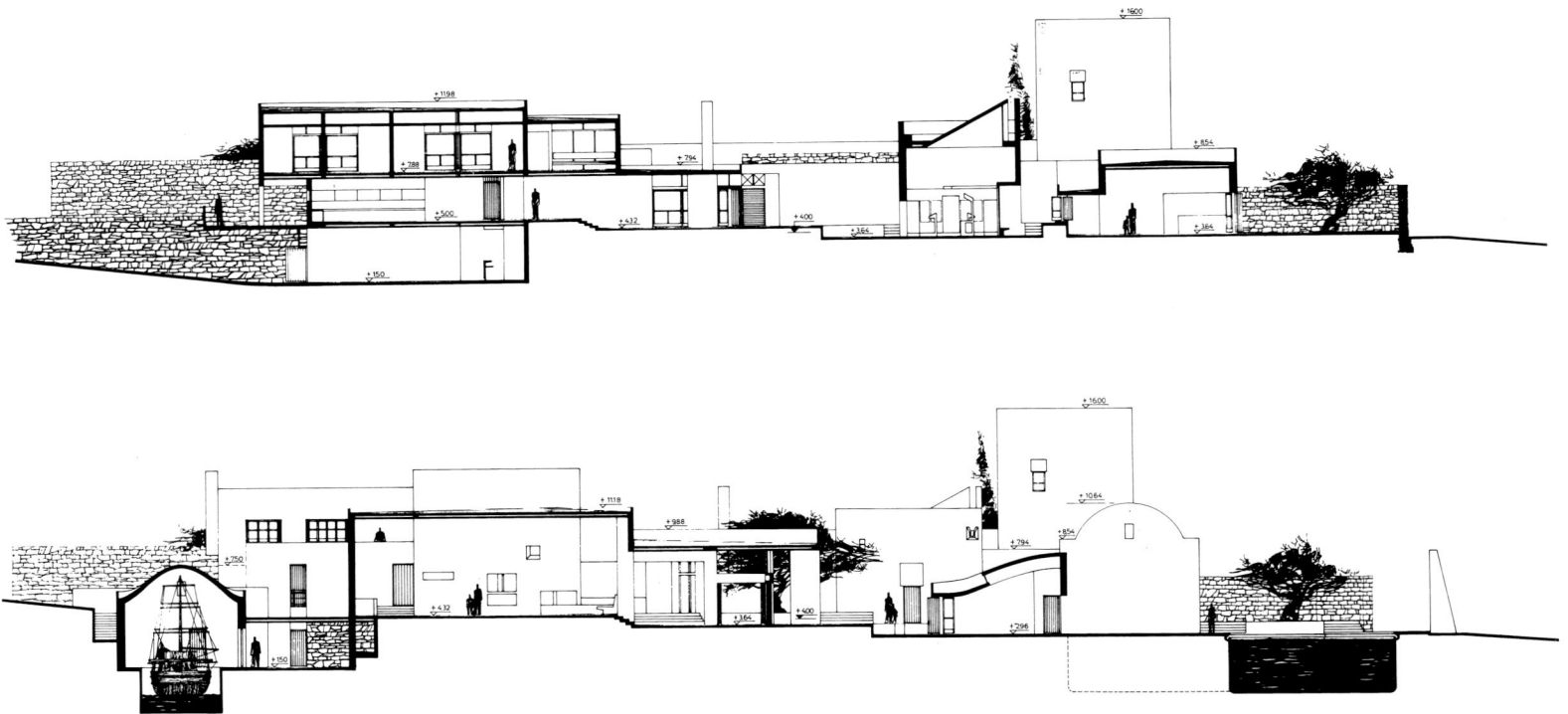

141

Different sections of the house.

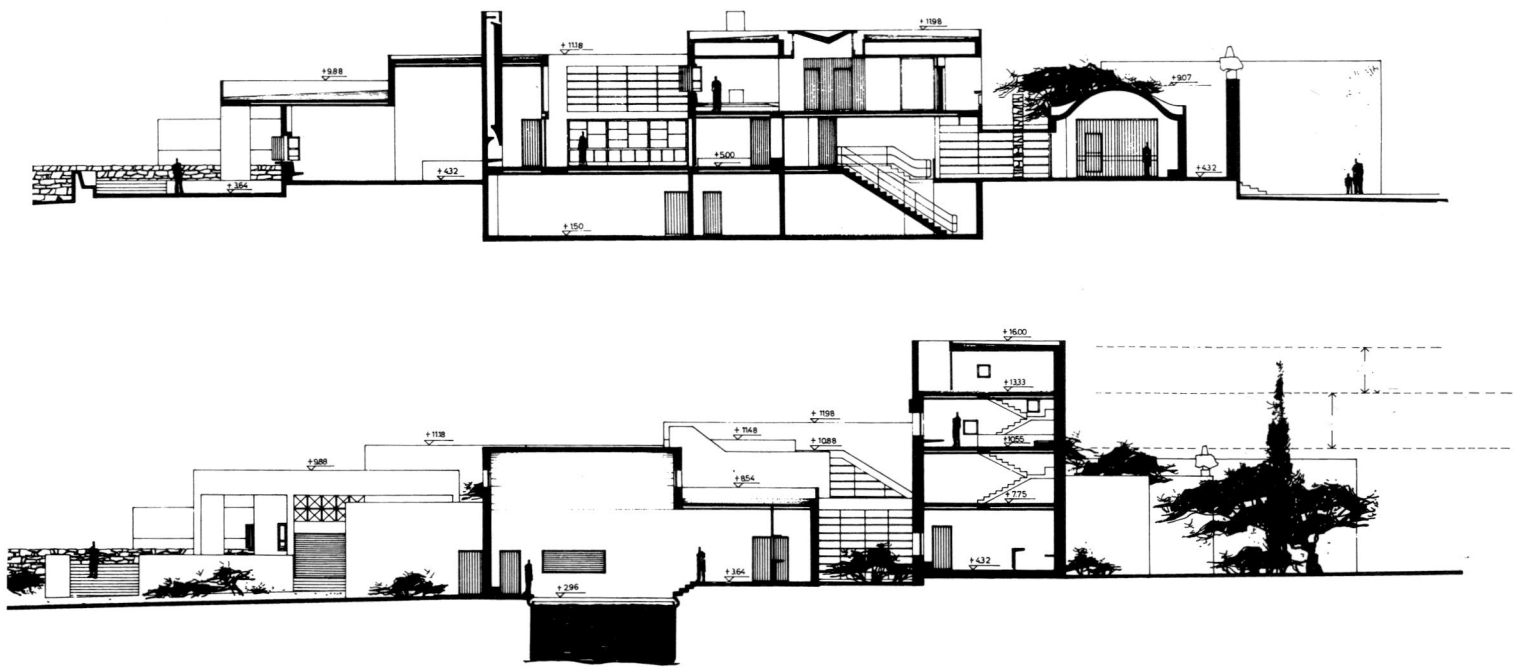

Panoramic view of the complex, showing the multitude of complementing surfaces.

143

This house in Chalcidice is laid out around a
central courtyard with a chapel in the centre.

particular artistic value. The constructions existing before
this date were extremely miserable, or were small
constructions attached to monasteries on the Mount of
Athos. The basic inspiration for these houses was the
configuration of the actual religious buildings to which
they were attached. These original buildings were
fortresses constructed around a central patio, with a
temple in the centre, which opened onto the sea.

These plans did not therefore pose any problem as far
as architectural style was concerned. Papayannopoulos
designed an important building and drew his inspiration
from the native morphology and style of the rich building
tradition of the Greek islands. Therefore, the architect set
out consciously to create a white house, to be
constructed on a large site located on a mall promontory,
which would benefit from the inherent simplicity of the
architecture of the Cycladic islands. At the same time, he
endeavoured not to fall into the easy folkloric style, which
migtht be expected in a project of this kind.

All of the above premises are incorporated into the
final design. The religious belief of the owners also gave a
certain direction to the project, and the house is laid out
like a Greek Orthodox monastery overlooking the sea.

However, Papayannopoulos had to find solutions to
overcome numerous problems caused by the unusual
configuration and large size of the site which the
residence was to occupy. These difficulties mainly
involved the resolution of volumetric problems and
deciding on the precise sizes and forms of the buildings
in the complex. In order to resolve these problems, the

144

The exterior design and interior layout of this house were based on the architecture of a Greek Orthodox monastery.

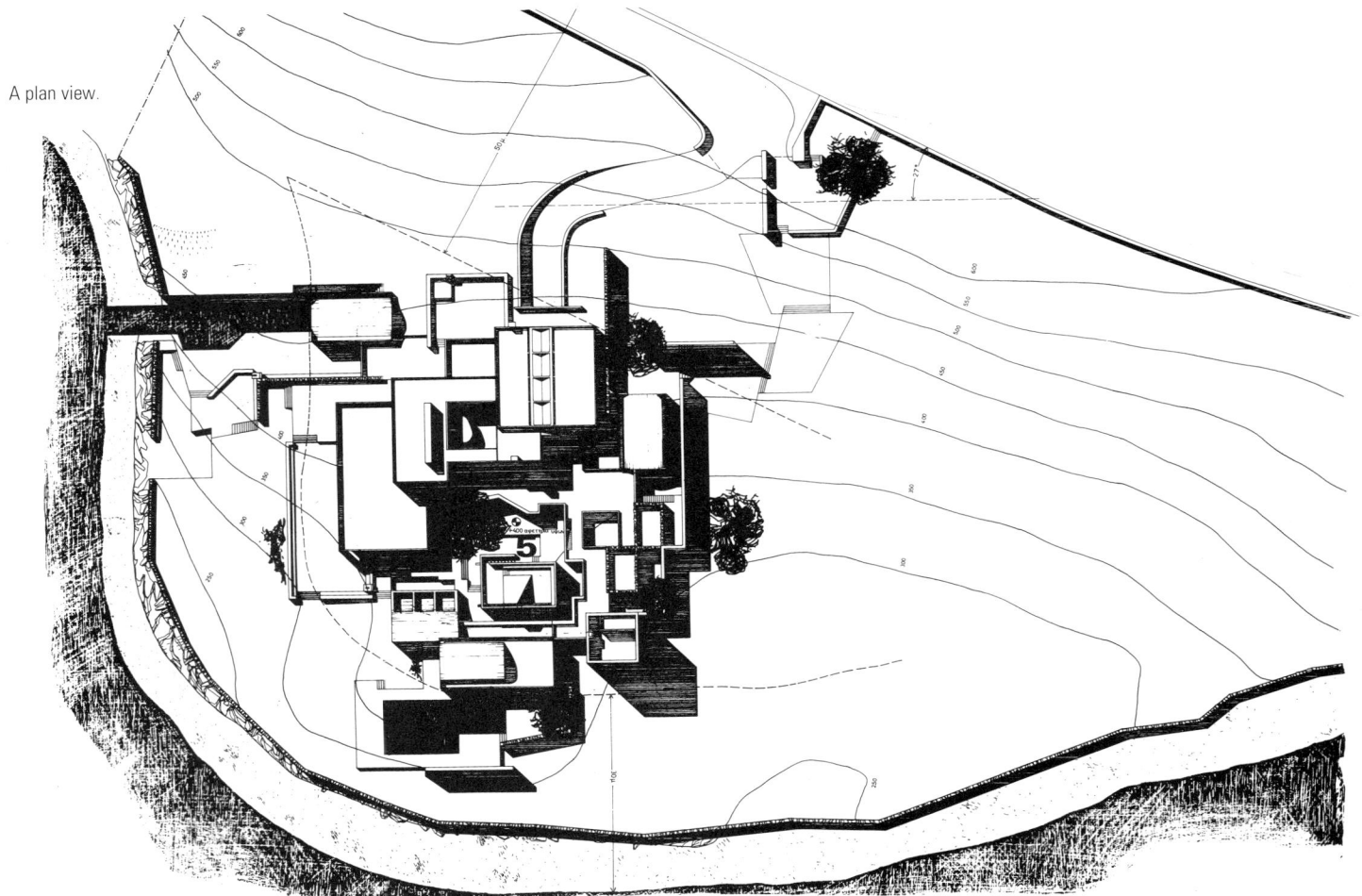

A plan view.

architect decided to group the rooms according to their functions, and make each one of these groupings a different height, while maintaining continuity between the different areas. This continuity was achieved, in many cases, by the creation of a number of atria. Similarly, the architect integrated the natural slope of the site into his design, thereby making possible different floor levels in different parts of the house.

Inspired by the religious constructions of these islands, the house in Chalcidice is laid out around a central courtyard, with a chapel in the centre. The entrance to the house is indirect, by means of a small hallway formed by two stone walls. The first room one enters is a vaulted construction with stone benches, a fireplace and a quiet place for visitors to sit. From here one can enter the hall, the auxiliary rooms (kitchen, storeroom, basement, etc.), and the guest rooms, as well as the all-season swimming pool and the crafts workshop. Further back there is a tower separated from the rest of the buildings in a quiet and peaceful setting.

A shipyard was built at sea level, and a slipway has been constructed, taking advantage of the natural slope of the land. The arsenal is beside a tavern and the dwelling's wine cellars. These areas are a continuation of the sitting rooms on the first floor. These is also a jetty where the fishermen can fix their nets, and eat and drink in the adjacent tavern.

The designer respected the natural slope of the land, and this allowed him to create different floor levels throughout the house.

Tapestries, bas-reliefs, fireplaces and other decorative elements were designed under Papayannopoulos' supervision.

The interior is characterised by its simplicity and the predominance of bright open spaces.

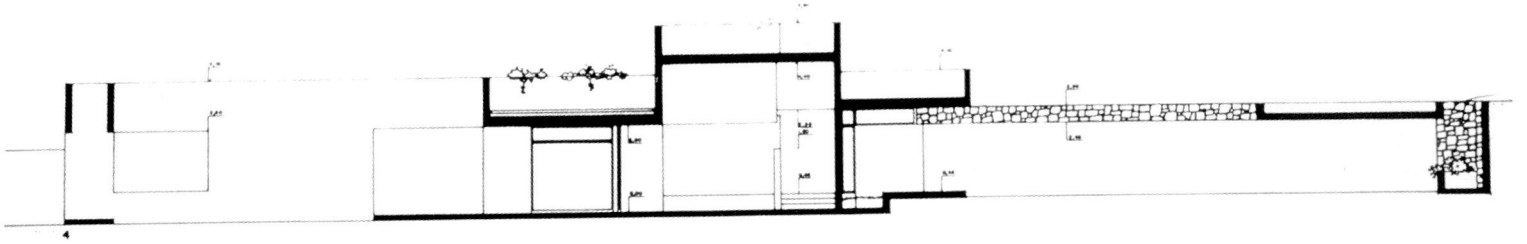

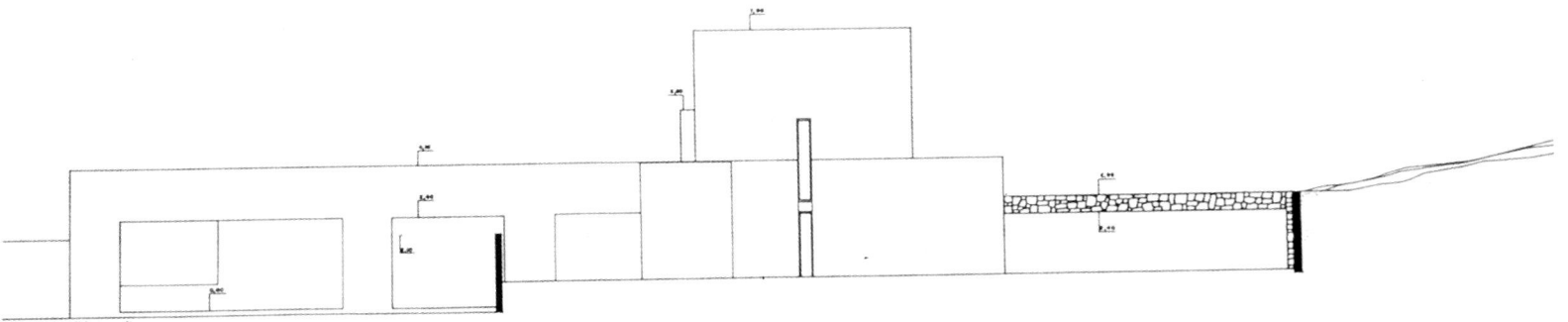

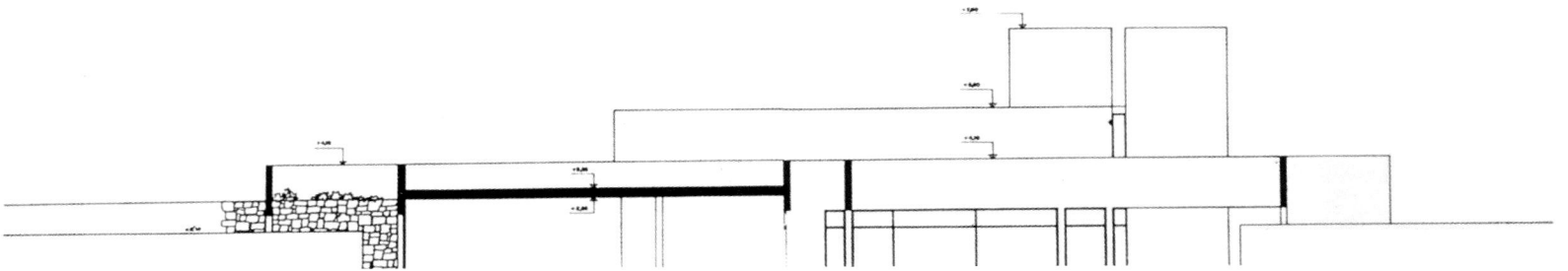

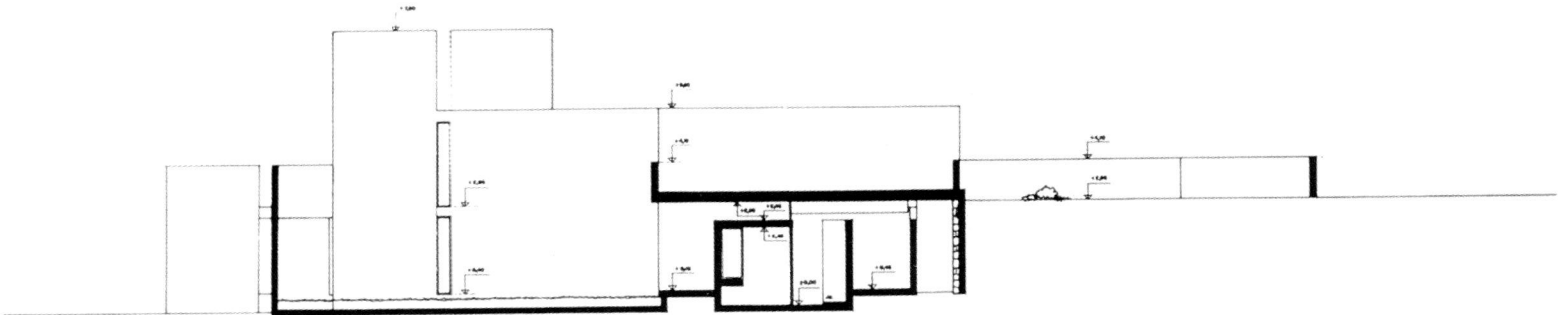

Different sections and elevations of the house.

White architecture

Enrique Álvarez-Sala, Carlos Rubio and Ignacio Vicens y Hualde

Single-family dwelling in Ibiza (Spain) by Enrique Álvarez-Sala, Carlos Rubio and Ignacio Vicens y Hualde.

As a memorial to other forms of white architecture down through the years, echoes deeply rooted in a past apparently not quite so dim and distant, this single-family dwelling by Enrique Álvarez-Sala, Carlos Rubio and Ignacio Vicens y Hualde is located at the very edge of the sea, and is designed as an essential, clear, contained geometric shape against a background of nature, always different, so beautiful, frugal, and dramatic.

This structure is to be found on the island of Ibiza, surrounded by the Mediterranean on the highest point of a hill, a pine forest at its back, with most of the property facing the sea. Thanks to the fact that the house is set on

the hill facing south, it provides some magnificent views of D'Alt Vila and the port of Ibiza.

Enrique Álvarez-Sala was born in Madrid in 1952. He graduated in architecture from Madrid's Escuela Técnica Superior de Arquitectura in 1977, and has lectured in construction in this establishment since 1983. He has won many prizes and honourable mentions, of which the most important are the following: first prize in a MOPU (Ministry of Public Works) competition involving the construction of country dwellings (Madrid, Spain, 1981), and first prize in a limited entry competition in Somosaguas (Madrid, Spain, 1985) run by the Vallehermoso SA firm, involving house construction.

Carlos Rubio was born in Barcelona in 1950. He graduated in architecture from the Escuela Técnica

151

View of the Catalan-style flat roof in brick, in
contrast to the finish of the white walls.